Heft 79 · Jahrgang 40 · Nummer 1/2024

Sünde und Schuld in einer nachchristlichen Gesellschaft

Barth verstehen und über ihn hinausgehen

Zeitschrift für Dialektische Theologie
Journal of Dialectical Theology

ISSN 0169-7536

Gründer
Gerrit Neven (Kampen)

Herausgeber
Georg Plasger (Siegen), Edward van 't Slot (Amsterdam) und Kait Dugan (Princeton)

Erweiterter Herausgeberkreis:
Gregor Etzelmüller (Osnabrück), Marco Hofheinz (Hannover), Bruce McCormack (Princeton), Günter Thomas (Bochum) und Matthias Wüthrich (Zürich)

Layout
Anna Lena Schwarz (Siegen)

Redaktionsanschrift
Universität Siegen
Prof. Dr. Georg Plasger
D - 57068 Siegen
zdth@uni-siegen.de

Abonnementskosten:
Preise inkl. MwSt.: Einzelheft & Einzelheft zur Fortsetzung: € 25,00, Rabatt für Mitglieder der Karl Barth-Gesellschaft e.V. & für Studierende: 25 %, jeweils zzgl. Versandkosten (Nachweis erforderlich). Die Fortsetzung läuft immer unbefristet, ist aber jederzeit kündbar.

Bestellservice: Leipziger Kommissions- und Großbuchhandelsgesellschaft (LKG)
An der Südspitze 1-12, 04579 Espenhain
Tel. +49 34206 65-116, Fax +49 34206 65-250. E-Mail: KS-team04@lkg.eu

© 2024 by Evangelische Verlagsanstalt GmbH · Leipzig
Printed in Germany

Das Werk einschließlich aller seiner Teile ist urheberrechtlich geschützt. Jede Verwertung außerhalb der Grenzen des Urheberrechtsgesetzes ist ohne Zustimmung des Verlags unzulässig und strafbar. Das gilt insbesondere für Vervielfältigungen, Übersetzungen, Mikroverfilmungen und die Einspeicherung und Verarbeitung in elektronischen Systemen.
Das Buch wurde auf alterungsbeständigem Papier gedruckt.

Cover: Kai-Michael Gustmann, Leipzig
Satz: Anna Lena Schwarz, Siegen
Drucken und Binden: Beltz Grafische Betriebe GmbH, Bad Langensalza
ISBN 978-3-374-07587-4
www.eva-leipzig.de

Inhalt / Content

Vorwort 5

Cornelis Christiaan den Hertog
Sin and Guilt in a Post-Christian Society: Understanding Barth and Thinking Beyond Him
Introducing the 40th International Karl Barth Conference 7

Cees-Jan Smits
Pride, Sloth, and Falsehood
Humanity As It Is Not According to Karl Barth 13

Aku Stephen Antombikums
"The Judge Judged in Our Place"
Sin and Atonement in Karl Barth 32

Jared Stacy
Agents of Reconciliation Amidst the Anthropocene
The Offer of Barth For The Church Facing Climate Crisis 48

Barth Graduate Student Colloquium (2023)

Morgan Bell
Rightly or Wrongly, Speaking the Father
Barth, Gender Performativity, and Patriological Analogy 65

Frank Della Torre II
Church and State in Barth's Political Theology 79

Joe Kauslick
Negation and Affirmation, Judgment, and Grace
Karl Barth's The Christian Life as a Theology of Christian Accountability 96

Eckhart Chan
The Compromise of Subordination
Tracing the "Positive" Theme in Barth's Church-State
Distinction 118

Enoch H. Kuo
Theology as Revisionary Political Philosophy
Thinking with Barth on Justification and Justice 136

Rezensionen / Reviews 157

Verzeichnis der Autoren 168

Vorwort

Sie halten hier eine neue Ausgabe der *Zeitschrift für Dialektische Theologie* in Händen – und sie enthält Beiträge, die bei verschiedenen Gelegenheiten präsentiert wurden.

Im Oktober 2023 organisierten einzelne niederländische Einrichtungen (Protestantisch-Theologische Universität, Theologische Universität Apeldoorn und die Fakultät Religion und Theologie der Freien Universität Amsterdam) die 40. Niederländische Karl Barth-Tagung. Das geschah zum zweiten Mal in Münster und zum dritten Mal vor allem in englischer Sprache. Thema war das Sündenverständnis Karl Barths, wobei aktuelle Fragen rund um das Thema Sünde und Schuld mit im Raum standen: Wie sprechen wir beispielsweise theologisch fruchtbar über kollektive Schuld angesichts der Klimakrise? Welche Rolle spielt Sünde im Trauma von Völkern, die sich gegen andere Völker erheben? Und kann man von Sünde sprechen, wenn Menschen aufgrund unterschiedlicher kultureller Erwartungen und Erfahrungen einander zu nahe treten (denken wir nur an die Genderdiskussion)?

In dieser Ausgabe finden Sie zunächst die Einleitung von Dr. Niels den Hertog (Theologische Universität Apeldoorn), die er zur Eröffnung der Konferenz gehalten hat. Es folgt ein Beitrag von Cees-Jan Smits (2020 an derselben Universität promoviert und regelmäßiger Besucher der Barth-Konferenzen), der deutlich macht, was heute in Barths Beschäftigung mit dem Sündenbegriff auf dem Spiel steht. 2023 hat Smits auf Niederländisch eine Einleitung über diese Thematik für ein größeres Publikum veröffentlicht; in seinem Beitrag hier in dieser Ausgabe geht er auf einzelne Akzente genauer ein.

Während der Konferenz hat eine Anzahl jüngerer Promovenden kleinere Vorträge über thematisch verwandte Problematiken gehalten. Zwei dieser Vorträge finden Sie hier abgeduckt; sie wurden durch Aku Antombikums (Amsterdam/Pretoria) und Jared Stacy (Bristol/Aberdeen) gehalten. Es lohnt sich zu sehen, wie Theologen aus verschiedenen Traditionen Gedanken aus der Dialektischen Theologie aufnehmen und sie auf ihre eigene Weise weiter zu denken versuchen.

Im englischsprachigen Bereich geschieht im Bereich der Barthforschung eine ganze Menge. Sie finden im weiteren Teil dieser Ausgabe Beiträge von Doktoranden, die am Barth Graduate Student Colloquium 2023 in Princeton interessante Vorträge über Barth und die Politik gehalten haben. Die Texte von Joe Kauslick (Boston), Enoch H. Kuo (Princeton), Morgan Bell (Toronto), Eckhart Chan (Oxford) und Frank Della Torre II (Baylor University) empfehlen wir Ihrer Lektüre; wir halten sie für geeignet, sie einer größeren Öffentlichkeit vorzulegen.

Und am Schluss finden Sie noch eine Rezension zum jüngst erschienenen Buch von Michael Weinrich mit dem Titel "Die eine heilige christliche und apostolische Kirche. Berufung und Sendung der Gemeinde", die von Dr. Reiner Dinger verfasst wurde.

Und gerne weisen wir zuletzt auch noch darauf hin, dass wir uns über deutsch- und englischsprachige Aufsätze im Bereich der Dialektischen Theologie freuen – wir ermuntern Sie deshalb gerne, uns Texte zuzusenden.

Wir wünschen Ihnen viel Lese- und Studienfreude!

Herzliche Grüße und für alle Herausgeber und Herausgeberinnen

Prof. Dr. Georg Plasger (Siegen) und Prof. Dr. Edward van 't Slot (PThU in den Niederlanden)

Cornelis Christiaan den Hertog

Sin and Guilt in a Post-Christian Society: Understanding Barth and Thinking Beyond Him

Introducing the 40th International Karl Barth Conference

> "There can, therefore, be no real faith in God which in the presence of the marvellous work of divine election and favour does not feel compelled to utter the cry of Peter in Luke 5:8: 'Depart from me; for I am a sinful man, O Lord.' Rightly understood, it is the believer and the believer alone who speaks in this way. For from grace and only from grace does the judgment proceed which compels a man to speak in this way. The man without grace and faith will not speak in this way. Rather he will attempt to evade the judgment and hide it from himself. […] In Scripture we do not find the Law alongside the Gospel but in the Gospel, and therefore the holiness of God is not side by side with but in His grace, and His wrath is not separate from but in His love."[1]

During the Dutch Barth Conference in Münster in October 2022, Barth's 1931 book *Fides quaerens intellectum* (FQI hereafter) was the subject of the conference discussion. FQI was the book in which Barth gives an account of what he considers a properly oriented theological method.[2] Barth's decisions in this book provides him the freedom to be fully and openly engaged as a theologian, without being constantly concerned with the question of whether he is concerned about the current state of affairs within society. In 1933, when many theologians in Germany were enthusiastically welcoming Hitler as a gift from God, Barth could say that he continued his work "as if nothing had happened" ("als wäre nichts geschehen").[3] But in the following year,

---
1 K. Barth, *CD II/1*, 359–60 (*KD II/1*, 407–8).
2 See Barth und Anselm (*Zeitschrift für Dialektische Theologie* 77, no.1 [2023]).
3 K. Barth, "Theologische Existenz Heute!" in Karl Barth, *Vorträge und kleinere Arbeiten 1930–1933*, ed. Michael Beintker, Michael Hüttenhoff, and Peter Zocher (Zürich: Theologischer Verlag Zürich, 2013), 271–363, 280.

Barth could also call the German church to its senses by putting forth to the synod his draft of what would become the *Barmer Thesen*, which were then adopted with only few amendments: the church knows no other source for its proclamation than the one Word spoken by God in Jesus Christ.

Yet this confession by no means halted developments in Germany, and in 1935, Barth was forced to leave Germany. One last word from Barth could still resound in October 1935 - but already, although he was present, no longer delivered by himself: *Gospel and Law* (*Evangelium und Gesetz*). Here Barth strongly refuted the classical Lutheran order of Law and Gospel, because he saw how unconcerned various theologians like Gogarten with his *volksnomos* were in thinking they could recognize the law in all kinds of other voices, in creation-order, or in the course of history. The night Barth delivered this lecture, he was expelled across the German-Swiss border and was not allowed to enter Germany for ten years. It was precisely this theology that concentrated entirely on its own matter and carried on "as if nothing had happened" that provided a critical potential during the first years of the Third Reich to speak clearly and decisively when it mattered.

In some ways, the 2023 Barth conference proceeded where the 2022 conference ended. Under the title "Sin and Guilt in a Post-Christian Society: Understanding Barth and Proceeding Beyond Him," the conference discussed Barth's teaching on sin. When Barth discusses sin in his *Church Dogmatics*, the decisions mentioned above from the 1930s were not forgotten.[4] It certainly is no coincidence that the first *Barmer These* returns when discussing Christ's prophetic ministry and the human lie (*CD IV/3*, 1). This means, unsurprisingly, that sin cannot be discussed properly apart from the gospel. Only in the light of Jesus Christ and his work can the true identity of humanity become clear. As obvious as this may sound, Barth implements here nothing short of a theological.[5] This bears equal novelty to shape of Barth's treatment of sin on the basis of the classic Reformed teaching of

---

4   This is not for the first time that Barth wrote about the doctrine of sin, but his most extensive treatment of the doctrine of the atonement doctrine can be found in *Church Dogmatics* IV, which he wrote in the 1950s.
5   Wolf Krötke, "Sünde und Nichtiges," in *Barth Handbuch*, ed. Michael Beintker (Tübingen: Mohr Siebeck, 2016), 342–7, 342. Michael Beintker, *Krisis und Gnade. Gesammelte Studien zu Karl Barth*, ed. Stefan Holtmann and Peter Zocher (Tübingen: Mohr Siebeck, 2013), 154. However, Beintker nuances the statement and says that Barth's teaching on sin "keineswegs so neu ist, wie mancher nach frischer Lektüre der Barthschen Versöhnungslehre gerne vermutet."

Christ's threefold ministry. In the light of Christ's work as King, Priest, and Prophet, the reality of the human identity is unveiled in their pride, sloth, and falsehood.

In the encounter with Jesus Christ, the human is revealed as a sinner. And at the same time, this encounter also revealed the reality of sin.[6] The in-depth and central core of sin is unbelief. Sin is the unbelief that this God means to do good towards God's creatures and that God knows what humans need. Sin is not primarily about a series of actions considered in isolation, but rather this primal decision that human beings want to live without this God. This affects the concrete actions of human beings and becomes visible in pride, slothfulness, and falsehoods. In using extensive exegetical excursions (all based on the Old Testament), Barth unpacks how this sin manifests itself in reality. Barth's frank and lucid insights on this topic are what still makes reading him on this subject today so compelling and fruitful.

In the meantime, one should not overlook the point that by making these choices, Barth refutes a long theological tradition which considered the knowledge of sin as knowledge that exists prior to and apart from the knowledge of Christ as Savior. The former could be learned from the Law and the second from the Gospel. This method could easily make knowledge of sin something of a condition for receiving the Gospel, and at the very least, it gave the impression that God speaks two words to this World: God's Law in which God first condemned the sinner and after this comes God's Gospel in which forgiveness is given to humanity. But Barmen declared that Jesus Christ is God's *one* Word. This certainly comes as *Zuspruch* and *Anspruch*, but they are *two* sides of the *one* Word, which is a critique of current reality. In reality, the one word breaks apart in a kind of prism into these two aspects, but this does not diminish its fundamental unity.

In the meantime, the following question resonates today and resonated during the conference: what about human reality? Precisely in thinking about the locus of sin is where one is tempted to think in terms of an *Anknüpfungspunkt* (a lead). As G.K. Chesterton remarked, the doctrine of original sin is the only Christian dogma that can be proven scientifically. Surely, most understand perfectly well what he meant? Newspapers are full of horrific injustice and suffering that people inflict on one another. The wars in Ukraine, Israel, and Gaza are all relevant examples of such injustice and

---

6   Paul Nimmo, "Karl Barth," in *T&T Clark Companion to the Doctrine of Sin*, ed. Keith T. Johnson and David Lauber (London: T&T Clark, 2018), 285–99, 286.

suffering, but there are also the wrongs in everyday interpersonal life that should be acknowledged. Human beings must reckon with the past. In terms of the Netherlands, the events in Indonesia and Dutch involvement in slave trading surface. If these painful realities will not be the starting point of our reflection, will we really be able to speak *zur Sache*?

Let us return to the beginning for a moment: confronted with Nazism, Barth's theology could clearly pinpoint the heart of the problem, and thus he inspired people in different countries to resist.[7] Though at first sight it seems appropriate to raise questions about that too. Why are the *Barmer Thesen* silent on what was already being done to Jews in Germany at that time (anti-Jewish measurements started as early as April 1933)? Is this not poignant evidence that by following his method, Barth eventually lost his sense of discernment for the harsh, sinful, and painful realities of this world? This is an important question, but one should not forget that already in October 1933, i.e., almost six months *before* Barmen, Barth asked his German colleagues the following question: why is the church silent about what is happening to the Jews?[8] For Barth, the answer to this question was clear: the church granted a legitimate place to other sources of knowledge within theology outside of God's one Word. This was the soil from which the errors of nationalism and anti-Semitism could grow. And to counter this error, it was necessary to return theologically matter-of-factly and soberly to this *one* question: where does humanity hear the voice of God? Barth *did* see things and did not remain silent. He looked for the *theological* question at stake in all this. And he answered it in a way that many understood at the time and gave many people courage to resist. Barth identified "The murky spring of a second revelation" ("Die trübe Quelle einer zweiten Offenbarung"),[9] as he called it, which claimed to provide theological knowledge apart from God's one Word

---

7   For instance, see Hans Joachim Iwand's review of CD I/1, in which he states the following regarding Barth's method: "daß aus dieser Burg Vorstöße kamen, die nicht nur dem Feinde Halt geboten, sondern auch manchen, der in Gefangenschaft geraten war, befreiten und wieder heimholten" ("that advances came from this castle, which not only stopped the enemy, but also freed some who had fallen into captivity and brought them home again") (H. J. Iwand, "Jenseits von Gesetz und Evangelium?," in *Um den rechten Glauben. Gesammelte Aufsätze*, trans. and ed. Karl Gerhard Steck (München: Chr. Kaiserverlag, 1959), 87–109, 89.

8   K. Barth, *Reformationstag 1933* (Zollikon: Evangelischer Verlag, 1998), 69.

9   K. Barth, "Bekenntnis der freien Kirchensynode, 1934," in Karl Barth, *Vorträge und kleinere Arbeiten 1934–1935*, ed. Michael Beintker, Michael Hüttenhoff, and Peter Zocher (Theologischer Verlag Zürich: Zürich, 2017), 60.

as the problem that was at stake in the confrontation with Anti-Semitism, racism, and the other atrocities of National socialism. If the Church took the Barmen Confession seriously, the church should and would have raised her voice against all injustice that was happening under Hitler's government.[10]

When discussing Barth's understanding of reality in his doctrine of sin, there is another point that should be considered. Barth developed his thought on sin during the years of reconstruction in Germany. Barth's dual insistence that 1) the human cannot have knowledge of their sin since they are a sinner (*KD IV/1*, 398) and that 2) only in the mirror of Jesus Christ does it become clear that the human being is a sinner and what their sin actually is (*KD IV/1*, 430) both become understandable if one read's about Barth's experiences in post-war Germany. During his first trip to Germany after the collapse of the Third Reich, Barth met with several colleagues who he thought shied away from taking responsibility for their involvement in Germany's guilt by constantly referring to demons who supposedly worked overtime during the Hitler-era. Barth asked them: "Why do you constantly refer to demons? Why don't you say concretely: we have been political fools? Please allow your Swiss colleague to exhort you to think more rationally!"[11] His firm focus on Jesus Christ alone as the source for human knowledge of sin saved Barth from being silenced when confronted with people who – like these German theologians – downplayed their responsibility and refused to accept the fact of their sin. Proper theology is not carried out by talking as

---

10   Barth, *Reformationstag 1933*, 68–9. See also Barth's input during the *Freie reformierte Synode* in Barmen-Gemarke (January 3rd and 4th 1934), which can be found in J. Beckmann, *Rheinische Bekenntnissynoden im Kirchenkampf. Eine Dokumentation aus den Jahren 1933–1945* (Neukirchener Verlag: Neukirchen-Vluyn, 1975): 34–46; Karl Barth, *Briefe des Jahres 1933. Herausgegeben von Eberhard Busch unter Mitarbeit von Bartolt Haase und Barbara Schenck* (Theologischer Verlag Zürich: Zürich, 2004), 502 (letter to Helmut Ehrenberg). For the discussion, see Eberhard Busch, *Unter dem Bogen des einen Bundes. Karl Barth und die Juden 1933–1945*, (Neukirchener Verlag: Neukirchen-Vluyn, 1996), 125–154.

11   K. Barth, "Und vergib uns unsere Schuld (14.9.1945)," in *Die Schuld der Kirche. Dokumente und Reflexionen zur Stuttgarter Schulderklärung vom 18./19. Oktober 1945*, Studienbücher zur kirchlichen Zeitgeschichte, Bd. 4, ed. Martin Greschat (Christian Kaiser Verlag: München, 1982), 81–85, 85. This seems to be the predominant issue on Barth's mind, because he also made mention of it in the report he wrote about his visit to the US military: "Bericht über eine Deutschlandreise, 19. August bis 4. September [1945], erstattet an die Organisation I der amerikanischen Armee in Deutschland" (in *Die evangelische Kirche nach dem Zusammenbruch. Berichte ausländischer Beobachter aus dem Jahre 1945*, ed. Clemens Vollnhals [Vandenhoeck & Ruprecht: Göttingen, 1988], 112–120, 115).

if the world the theologian addresses has no idea whatsoever about being a sinful world. By proclaiming Jesus Christ and his victory over sin, theology can reveal what otherwise would remain hidden. This theology has great potential in unmasking perpetrators who consider themselves victims of larger forces rather than the sinners they are. It does not wait for the sinner to consider themselves a sinner. Rather, this theology confidently calls people to the truth about themselves which is revealed in the work of Jesus Christ. The problem at stake turns out not to be whether human beings ever *get* to reality if they start from God's revelation in Jesus Christ. Humanity faces a much deeper problem: apart from Jesus Christ, humanity has no access to reality. It is not as if humanity knows reality and the only problem is to connect reality with Jesus Christ. The opposite is true: in the encounter with Jesus Christ, humanity gains access to the world as it really is.

This does not mean that questions cannot or should not be asked. Even if this theology is enjoyed for providing joyful frankness in addressing sinners, one can still raise the question regarding what theology only knows about *forgiven* sin (KD II/2, 860) should mean for victims of this world. Can this do justice to the unjust pain and suffering in the world? As much as Barth's approach gave him preeminent space to hold perpetrators accountable, it cannot be ruled out that their victims, many of whose relatives did not survive the war, would struggle with the unintended effect that Barth's talk of *forgiven* sin had on them. What if these victims of injustice were unable to forgive? Would God forgive these particular victims regardless of whether they had forgiven their perpetrator?

In the face of the ongoing and current intensifying injustice of war, violence, racism, and antisemitism, these are critical and serious questions. These dark realities force theologians to say things differently than Barth in his days. Even if this is true, deep engagement with his theology is beneficial. The theologian does not need to become a Barthian, but theologians must be *good* theologians. The task before theologians today is not to look for a quick message with which to give one's political opinion, but rather asking continually: what is really happening here? What is at stake?

Cees-Jan Smits

Pride, Sloth, and Falsehood

Humanity As It Is Not According to Karl Barth

Karl Barth wrote his hamartiology in the 1950s. Those were the years of "shock," as Eberhard Busch points out in his article on Barth's doctrine of sin.[1] Or at least it should have been the years of shock, because the full extent of the Holocaust could no longer be denied. But as Busch cites Barth, "it didn't convince us of our lostness and damnation in such a way that we couldn't escape it anymore."[2]

---

1   The following is some literature on Karl Barth's doctrine of sin, in order of appearance: William David Ellington, "Karl Barth's Doctrine of Sin in the Church Dogmatics Volumes I/-IV/3," PhD diss, (Boston University Graduate School, 1965); Wolf Krötke, *Sünde und Nichtiges bei Karl Barth*, (Leipzig: Evangelische Verlagsanstalt, 1970); Eberhard Busch, "Die Entlarvung der Sünde im Licht ihrer Überwindung. Karl Barths Sündenlehre," *Zeitschrift für Dialektische Theologie* 6, no. 2 (1990): 109–32; Jan Taeke Bakker, "Die Sünde in der Kirchlichen Dogmatik. Höhepunkte aus der Sündenlehre Karl Barths," *Zeitschrift für Dialektische Theologie* 9, no.1 (1993): 9–19; Carlo Johan Willem Leget, "Quanti ponderis sit peccatum. Sündenverständnis nach Karl Barth und Thomas von Aquin, ein Vergleich," *Zeitschrift für Dialektische Theologie* 9, no. 1 (1993): 49–58; Matthias D. Wüthrich, *Gott und das Nichtige. Zur Rede vom Nichtigen ausgehend von Karl Barths KD § 50* (Zürich: Theologischer Verlag Zürich, 2006); Matt Jenson, *The Gravity of Sin: Augustine, Luther, and Barth on 'Homo Incurvatus in se'* (London: T&T Clark, 2006); Michael Beintker, "Hamartiologie und Christologie. Die Bauformen der Sündenlehre in KD IV/1–3," *Zeitschrift für Dialektische Theologie* 27, no. 1 (2011): 39–59; Wolf Krötke, "Sünde und Nichtiges," in *Barth Handbuch*, ed. Michael Beintker (Tübingen: Mohr Siebeck, 2016), 342–7; Matt Jenson, "Barth on Sin," in *The Wiley Blackwell Companion to Karl Barth, Volume I: Barth and Dogmatics*, ed. George Hunsinger and Keith L. Johnson (Hoboken, NJ: Wiley Blackwell, 2020), 197–206; Shao Kai Tseng, *Barth's Ontology of Sin and Grace: Variations on a Theme of Augustine* (London: Routledge, 2020); Cees-Jan Smits, *Veroordeeld tot genade. In gesprek met Karl Barth over de zonde* (Baarn: Willem de Zwijgerstichting, 2023).

2   Karl Barth, *Die christliche Lehre nach dem Heidelberger Katechismus* (Zollikon: Evangelischer Verlag, 1948), 48–49.

This direct context should indeed be taken into account when Barth's doctrine of sin is examined roughly seventy years after it was written.[3] Barth did not write in a vacuum, and Busch convincingly shows that those critics who blamed Barth for writing a "harmless" hamartiology were really missing the mark. Barth pursued a "harmful" doctrine of sin, which sought to convince his contemporaries of lostness and damnation outside Christ.

But on the other hand, Barth did not write for or within a confined area of only a few decades either. His doctrine of sin is not limited to dealing with recent horrors from a theological perspective. In fact, these horrors are hardly even mentioned in the many pages of Barth's hamartiology. As always, Barth goes beyond the "bad fruits," down to what he perceives to be the "bad tree"; he aims at establishing a discourse with modernity, including those deep convictions at its roots which eventually could be said to have led to such atrocities as the Holocaust.

Regarding sin, no one in modernity did more to discredit the Christian concept of sin than Friedrich Nietzsche. Since Spinoza, the concept of sin had been problematic. But Nietzsche doubled down on Spinoza's view – in the end, the concept of sin, in his view, fatally crippled and weakened humanity. If human persons were to be saved, they were to be saved from the mistaken and even sick idea of their own sinfulness. They should regain their honor and live royally, hailing the Übermensch.

Barth was very aware of Nietzsche's views of sin, and Barth critically engages Niezsche extensively in CD III/2, §45.2. Here Barth confronts Nietzsche's understanding of humanity through a theological anthropology that takes Christ as the sole representative of real humanity. Christ has shown the true meaning of being a human. And it is this anthropology which, in turn, serves as the background against which Barth discusses the dark features of sin. Sin is aversion from the humanity that God offers us in Christ: sin is everything which goes against God, in whom humble, royal, and true life is to be found, and which God freely gives to us.

Barth works through this point in depth in part four of his *Church Dogmatics*, which has reconciliation as its main theme. Volume CD IV/1 is about the descent of Christ who is the Son of God. This descent reveals, according to Barth, humanity's pride (*Hochmut*, § 60). CD IV/2 is about the ascent of

---

3   This essay is an extended version of my basic introductory paper for the 40th International Karl Barth conference in Münster in 2023 on the topic of sin and guilt in a post-Christian Society.

Christ who is the Son of Man. This ascent reveals humanity's sloth (*Trägheit*, § 65). CD IV/3 has a different scope – it examines Christ's testimony, which reveals humanity's falsehood (*Lüge*, § 70). These three features of pride, sloth, and falsehood are the three focal points of Barth's doctrine of sin. Together, they open up an entrance gate for the invasion of nothingness (*Das Nichtige*) into creation, which Barth already discussed in CD III/3. Nothingness is something akin to the "ground" of sin, which is however, according to Barth, "groundless."

In this general introduction, separate attention must be given to Barth's three preliminary sections (§ 60.1, § 65.1, and § 70.1) in which he establishes his starting point. Second, pride and sloth are to be dealt with. They belong together, because they mirror one another. The third section is on falsehood, by which human beings damn themselves to live by their own sinful systems, either religious or secular. Finally, this essay will discuss sin and nothingness. Difficult questions of ontology come into play here, but the confines of this essay prohibit an in-depth engagement of the topic beyond passing remarks.

Every part of this essay will start with a nod to Friedrich Nietzsche; not to contrast him extensively with Barth for his own sake, but for the purpose of highlighting the background against which Barth is operating.

1. The Starting Point

Sin is a theological category, which implies a belief in a God against whom sins are committed. The notion of sin can only be a meaningful concept inside the context of faith; in secular culture, sin serves as a light-hearted metaphor for anything one finds annoying or even appetizing ("guilty pleasures").

This is very clear from Nietzsche. In the end, according to Barth, he did not care much about denying the existence of God.[4] But he did care much about denying the nihilistic theories surrounding belief in God, foremost of all the doctrine of sin. For Nietzsche, sin doesn't exist at all, and this should be proven thoroughly. In his *Genealogy of Morality* he goes on to show at length how good and evil are nothing but social-cultural-political concepts, referring not to the will of God, nor to any metaphysical order, but (beneath a religious surface), exactly to what benefits a person or group of people and

---

4   Barth, *KD III/2*, 285 (footnotes to the *Church Dogmatics* refer to the German original *Kirchliche Dogmatik*).

what does not.⁵ Sin is not that which goes against the "grain of the universe," but simply that which some people find undesirable behaviour. There is no transcendent, absolute measure of good and evil. Moral talk of law and deviation from law just protects the interests of those in charge. The language of sin, then, came into being primordially to protect the interests of priests and temples. But there is no such thing as sin as such, for there is no moral law as such. Morality always just comes down to politics.

Surprisingly, Barth seems to agree. He begins his doctrine of sin by pointing out extensively that humanity cannot measure sin over against some law, either natural or one supposedly revealed in Scripture.⁶ Whenever humanity does try to attach sin to a specific law, humanity should be aware of hidden political interests. Barth's battle with natural theology is fought on this front as well, and he uses two excursions to substantiate his general thesis on the rise and fall of modern Protestant theology in this respect.⁷ Just as the law should not come prior to the gospel, but only follow as the outward "form" of the gospel, so sin too cannot be measured to any independent law outside the law as fulfilled in Christ. The "iron structure" of gospel preceding law sets out the guidelines here as elsewhere in the *Church Dogmatics*.⁸

Hamartiology should not be grounded then, according to Barth, in morality. It should be grounded in Christ. Whether or not human creatures are sinners should not be distinguished by any set of given prescriptions, but by the kind of humanity encountered as being invested with authority. Sin is elusive indeed. It cannot easily be grasped. But as soon as human beings begin with belief in Jesus Christ, they cannot help but to begin speaking about sin. The revelation of Christ means the revelation of sin as well. In fact, according to Barth in § 60.1, the humble coming of Christ judges humanity on four counts, and, in § 65.1, the royal coming of Christ shames us on four counts. The Christ event judges us, because it confronts us with divine humility, in which God keeps the covenant to the point of taking death upon Himself.

---

5   F. W. Nietzsche, *On the Genealogy of Morality: A Polemic* (1887), first treatise.
6   Barth, *KD IV/1*, 396–430.
7   Barth, *KD IV/1*, 407–11 on reformed orthodoxy, 413–27 on liberal protestantism.
8   Barth, *KD IV/3*, 427–428; cf. Eberhard Jüngel, "Evangelium und Gesetz. Zugleich zum Verhältnis von Dogmatik und Ethik," in idem, *Barth-Studien* (Gütersloh: Benzinger u. Mohn, 1982), 180–209, 180: "Die Umkehrung der traditionellen Reihenfolge ist von höchster Bedeutung für alles, was in der Kirchlichen Dogmatik an materialer Dogmatik vorgetragen wird. Das mit der Reihenfolge 'Evangelium und Gesetz' angemeldete theologische Programm entscheidet über die Gotteslehre, über die Anthropologie und über die Lehre von der Sünde."

This clearly shows 1) sin exists, 2) sin is reprehensible, 3) sin is true of all of us, and 4) sin has enormous weight.⁹ And the Christ event shames humanity, because it confronts human beings with the reality of what humanity could be like, as Christ keeps the covenant to the point of fully giving himself in obedience. This shows 1) humanity differs from Christ, 2) which is shameful, 3) for all of us, 4) and which should not be taken lightly.¹⁰ Not any separate law, but the humble and royal coming of Christ is God's judgment upon us, in which God reveals human sinfulness.

Thus, for Barth, Christ is the measure of sin. He is *vere deus*, showing how humble God really is, in whose image human beings have been created. And Christ is *vere homo*, "normal" man, revealing how human beings have become abnormal, not fully human. In Christ, humanity sees what true divinity and humanity are like: being humble, yet royal and true at the same time, and keeping the covenant. Just like "analogy" is the guiding principle which gives coherence to the positive theological statements in the *Church Dogmatics* as a whole, so "difference," or "dissimilarity," or "incongruity" is its counterpart used for that which does *not* positively cohere with Christ but is inversely proportional to him.¹¹

Barth keenly senses here how modernity as a whole, not just with Nietzsche, has fundamental suspicions about the Christian message that humans are sinners. However, it is not clear that modern human beings should be. When one looks around today, one sees ordinary people, living ordinary lives, and most are not hurting anyone. In the 1950s, ordinary people could have caused more severe hurt only a few years earlier, but still Barth concedes the point. Perhaps some harbor hate and animosity. Others may occasionally come across as blasphemous. But is it really clear that human beings are sinners? Of course, people make mistakes and may be flawed, but human beings cannot know everything. Barth points out that some even go further and argue that the transgressor might even be the true, free, and courageous individual, e.g., Prometheus who stole fire from the gods, Nietzsche's Übermensch who transcends good and evil, etc..¹² Are not those the heroes of humanity?

---

9   Barth, *KD IV/1*, 439–58.
10 Barth, *KD IV/2*, 436–52.
11 Cf. E. Jüngel, "Die Möglichkeit theologischer Anthropologie auf dem Grunde der Analogie. Eine Untersuchung zum Analogieverständnis Karl Barths," in *Barth-Studien*, 210–32.
12 Barth, *KD IV/1*, 443.

By pointing out these objections, Barth shows that the real question underlying the doctrine of sin is the standard by which real humanity is measured. For Barth, humanity is judged by the event in which God turned Godself towards humanity in gracious compassion to keep the covenant in Christ. No one is truly human like Christ. His humanity authoritatively reminds humanity of its origin. In Christ, humanity does not merely face an individual but the "True Human" who is completely at one with God. Christ is the prototype of humanity who is closer to human beings than they are to themselves, and Christ is the one who confronts humanity with its destiny. Thus, if this humble, silent Lamb – who is also the royal Lion of Judah – has been crucified, then such an event has critical consequences for humanity. Beyond and amid ordinary human life, there is a persistent will to break free from the covenant. The fate suffered by Jesus Christ then unmistakably reveals a dark truth about humanity and testifies to a hidden urge for the expulsion of God, fratricide, and self-hatred, all in one.[13] For in Christ, humanity meets not only *vere homo*, but *vere deus* and humanity's own *imago* as well.

The human aversion from its source happens continually, but it reached a climax in the life and death of Christ. Sin was revealing its true nature over against Christ. Sin has faced a climactic showdown, and thereby sin has lost all its evasiveness and elusiveness. From this vantage point, sin can be given its proper names. According to Barth, the climactic showdown of sin in the Christ event illuminates the hidden tracks of sin in ordinary life. By rejecting Christ, sin has revealed itself as pride, sloth, and falsehood. Pride and sloth, as Barth discusses in Church Dogmatics IV/1–2, mirror one another.

2. Pride and Sloth

Sin does not exist, according to Nietzsche, but talk about sin does exist, and it exists for a reason, which he goes on to demonstrate in the *Genealogy of Morality*.[14] Religious talk about good and evil was invented for a specific purpose: to protect the interests of the *weak*. What is called evil is that which is strong, from the perspective of the weak: the landlord raping one's wife, laying down high taxes, or killing at will. Praise for justice and mercy tends always to come "from below," not from those profiting from injustice and mercilessness. Morality is lower class people striking back at higher class

---

13 Barth, *KD IV/1*, 441–442.
14 Nietzsche, *Genealogy of Morality*, first treatise.

people by burdening the latter with a conscience. Christian talk about pride as a negative action only shows the higher class has nothing to be proud of – or so Nietzsche would want to say.

The architecture of Barth's hamartiology almost seems to be designed as a refutation of Nietzsche. At the start of CD IV/2 § 65.2, Barth acknowledges that Christian talk about sin has too often focused solely on "high" kinds of sin indeed: pride, arrogance, secular detached intelligence, etc. The following is a quote to illuminate the far-ranging importance this has for Barth:

> "In Protestantism and perhaps in Western Christianity in general, we are tempted to overlook this side of the matter or at least underestimate its importance. What we are interested in is Prometheus, who wants to snatch his thunderbolt from Zeus: the man who wants to be like God. We should be interested in this figure indeed and always make clear to ourselves how powerfully it is contradicted by God's grace. But the man of sin is not only this rebel, and his sin not only has this heroic form, in which one also has certain features of a dark beauty! You can easily see past yourself if you constantly want to understand your sin as *hubris*. Man's sin is not only heroic, but also ordinary, trivial, banal evil. He is not just Prometheus or Lucifer, but also quite simply a lazy person, a dormouse, a loiterer, a sloth. He exists not only in an evil above, but also (in the strange unity and reciprocity of these two seemingly opposite determinations) in an equally evil below. As there he is in dire need of humiliation, so here he is in dire need of elevation."[15]

So for Barth, Christ constitutes a righteous "middle" between "high" and "low" kinds of sin. Sin is twofold; and ordinary, passive, negligent kinds of sin should not be magnanimously excused but rather addressed as clearly as active strife and contention. Barth is in good Aristotelian company here: virtue is able to keep measure, and vice is diverting on either side.[16]

Therefore, after establishing his starting point, Barth proceeds with a parallel discussion in § 60.2 and § 65.2. These two paragraphs, each containing four large sections, together make for the heart of Barth's hamartiology, by far occupying the largest number of pages. They do not come from nowhere but have their roots in Barth's doctrine of creation and doctrine of God.

---

15 Barth, *KD IV/2*, 453.
16 Aristotle, *Nicomachean Ethics*, ed. and trans. E. Rackham (Cambridge, MA: Harvard University Press), 1926, II, 8: "There are then three dispositions – two vices, one of excess and one of defect, and one virtue which is the observance of the mean; and each of them is in a certain way opposed to both the others. For the extreme states are the opposite both of the middle state and of each other, and the middle state is the opposite of both extremes."

In CD IV/1, the four perspectives entail a movement of the human heart which could be called "upward," and which goes against the downward, humble movement God makes for humanity's benefit and justification, keeping the covenant in Christ. God has chosen to humbly take humanity's burden upon Godself, as Barth says in his doctrine of election (CD II/2). However, humanity tries to be like God whereas Christ became man; humanity tries to be lord whereas Christ became humanity's servant. Humanity attempts to judge whereas Christ was judged; humanity tries to save itself whereas Christ gave himself over for humanity. Thus, Barth's hamartiology in § 60.2 should be read against the background of God's eternal decision to humbly keep the covenant with humanity.

In CD IV/2, four new perspectives come to the fore, which entail a downward movement of the human heart that goes against how God aims to sanctify humanity. This part of Barth's discussion is grounded in CD III/2 and CD III/4, where he examined what real humanity looks like. Nietzsche is one of his main counterparts in this discussion. Real humanity cannot be found in heroic solitude, but rather in free and loving relationality, corresponding as the *imago Dei* to God's own free and loving relationality (CD II/1). For humanity, this has four dimensions, as Barth points out in CD III/2: towards God (§ 44), towards fellow humans (§ 45), towards humans themselves (§ 46), and towards human time (§ 47). Every dimension comes with a corresponding command of God as creator in CD III/4, which shows humanity how to live in freedom for God (§ 53), freedom in community (§ 54), freedom for life (§ 55), and freedom within boundaries (§ 56). In § 65.2, these same four dimensions return once more. Contrary to humanity's true calling, human beings live in stupidity in relation to God (*Dummheit*) whereas Christ listens to God. Humanity lives inhumanely in relation to fellow humans (*Unmenschlichkeit*) whereas Christ is fully human. Humanity lives with the dissipation of mind and body in relation to themselves (*Verlotterung*) whereas Christ is one. Humanity lives with fear in relation to its natural end (*Sorge*) whereas Christ is free.

In this way, Barth places sin in the spotlight of these eight perspectives, which are firmly embedded in other parts of the *Church Dogmatics*. At the same time, it would not be difficult to relate these perspectives to the eight or seven deadly sins known from the Christian tradition with pride, wrath, eagerness, and envy on one side, and greed, lust, gluttony, and sloth on the other.

Finally, it is important to note that CD IV/1 and CD IV/2 also mirror one another on this point. The sin of sloth is not a second sin next to the sin of pride, but they are the other side of the same coin. Pride always comes with sloth in another part of human existence, and sloth always comes with pride (e.g., being too proud to study, because "I know that already"). Just as Christ is fully one in his humiliation and exaltation, so humanity is one in its pride and sloth.

This seems to be how Barth would answer Nietzsche. Christianity does not advocate sloppiness and mediocrity against aristocracy. On the contrary, Christianity also pins down sloth as a sinful resistance of the calling to resemble true humanity in Christ. Christ is not only humble – he is also royal. Neglecting humanity's call to be fully human is nothing but sin.

	IV/1	IV/2	IV/3
Act of God:	Christ the Son of God as humble Priest	Christ the Son of Man as exalted King	Christ the faithful Prophet
Keeping the covenant by moving	Downward as God	Upward with man	Outward to all creation
Sin as most important feature of *nothingness* (III/3) Prolegomena to hamartiology (§ **60.1**, § **65.1**, § **70.1**)			

Act of Sin:	§60.2: Pride (Active)	§65.2: Sloth (Passive)	§ 70.2: Falsehood (Communicating)
Breaking the covenant	Not being human as set out by Christ the Son of God (§ II/2)	Not being human as set out by Christ the Son of Man (§ III/2 > III/4)	Locking out the Gospel (§ I/1)
By moving	Upward 1. Trying to be like God whereas Christ became human 2. Trying to be lord whereas Christ is servant 3. Trying to judge whereas Christ is judged	Downward 1. Stupidity in relation to God whereas Christ is listening 2. Inhumanity in relation to fellow humans whereas Christ is human 3. Dissipation of mind and body whereas Christ is one 4. Fear in relation to humanity's natural end whereas Christ is free § 65.3 Misery	Inward 1. As church in doctrinal systems 2. As world in ideological systems whereas Christ is the crucified yet risen Lord, transcending all systems
Terminating in	4. Humanity trying to save itself whereas Christ gave himself § 60.3 Fall	4. Fear in relation to humanity's natural end whereas Christ is free § 65.3 Misery	§ 70.3 Damnation

What stands out is *how* Barth discusses each of these eight perspectives. In every section, he makes the same kind of circle around the aspect of sin being discussed. This circle consists of four distinct steps. Barth painstakingly walks them again and again, so this seems to be his *röntgen* device interrogating the inner dynamic of sin.

In his first step, Barth points out that all kinds of sin are always *futile*. Sin can never achieve what it wants. For example, on the side of pride: while God could descend from heaven to become human, humanity cannot hope to ascend to heaven to become God. Or on the side of sloth: even in humanity's greatest stupidity, it will never succeed in extinguishing the light of God's wisdom in Christ. Every aspect of sin is futile, because God has acted against it and conquered sin in Christ. Darkness can do nothing against light, or as Barth remarks in CD IV/3 with a popular saying: "A lie has short legs."

In his second step, Barth points out that every kind of sin nevertheless is real and *factual*, although it is *without proper reason*. Sin exists as a *brutum factum*. Futile as sin is, it still has many grave consequences, which makes sin very dangerous. Those trying to become Lord may not succeed, because only Christ is Lord, but still, they leave a trail of destruction behind them by making all kinds of victims. While the humble Christ uplifts the weak, human pride belittles the weak and makes them cry out towards heaven. This is true of all aspects of sin as well. Every aspect of sin causes its own kind of damage – in humanity's relationship with God, with fellow humans, between mind and body, and, as one might want to add nowadays, in the human climate. Barth stresses the irrationality of all this. Of course, pride and sloth always have their excuses, but in the end, human beings are proud and banal for no reason. There is no proper ground to humanity's sinful acts. Human beings just sin because they sin, and from nothing, so it seems.

The third step is where Barth highlights how each kind of sin tries to cover itself. Sin never shows itself as sin, but it always provides a guise, which seems to excuse or even justify it. Humanity always rationalizes its sinful actions, giving them other names. Humanity justifies pride as self-preservation, individuality, or even as a moral responsibility. Humanity calls inhumanity healthy pragmatism, lust is conceived as not being Victorian and listening to humanity's natural impulses, and fear is understood as taking proper measures in advance. Every vice has its specific justification, and Barth is instructive in calling things for what they are in reality.

The fourth step entails how human beings always make fatal mistakes in sinning, which will cost humanity dearly. Human beings are mistaken about

God, about themselves, about their fellow humans, and about what humanity is doing. In trying to be God, humanity suspects God to be a threat to human autonomy, whereas God is actually the source of human freedom. In belittling fellow humans, humanity fatally underestimates its interdependence. Human pride and human sloth destroy what could have healed humanity with love and proximity.

As such, for Barth, sin is a movement of the heart which goes against God's movement towards humanity. God humbles Godself to uplift humanity, but humanity is proud and unwilling to be uplifted. When seen in light of the Christ event, this is what is at stake in ordinary human life. In and through ordinary life, humanity relates to God's movement to keep God's side of the covenant. Human deeds and negligence do not stand on their own, but they are the outward appearance of humanity's inward stance towards its part of the covenant. There is always a kind of relating to God in Christ involved in it and "sin" is the judgment upon turning one's back to God. Human beings do not accomplish anything with it, but instead they cause a great deal of damage. Human beings justify themselves, but in reality, they make fatal mistakes.

As Barth discusses in the concluding sections § 60.3 and § 65.3, this act of sin both *terminates in and comes from* the reality of being under sin: "Our second section provided us with an answer to the question what human sin is like. Now we have to answer the question who the sinner is, who does sin."[17] Just as act and being are one for God, so too human act and human being are fundamentally one, even though God steps in with God's reconciling act to free humanity from being under sin.

As the proverb has it, pride terminates in the fall, and sloth terminates in misery. Humanity's reasoning becomes darkened, it deprives itself of its freedom and its affections become unbridled. Breaking the covenant involves accumulating an ever-growing debt, burdening humanity with an ever-greater guilt, and then deteriorating to the point of complete corruption. Humanity is in dire need of salvation. By existing as God's outward event of grace to all creation, Christ himself testifies that this salvation is at hand. But such is the power of sin that humanity does not even want this good news to be true. This is what Barth emphasizes in his third part on sin.

---

17 Barth, *KD IV/1*, 531.

3. Falsehood

Nietzsche anticipated what would happen when humanity becomes aware of the death of God, in his vivid portrayal of the madman on the market:

> "Who gave us the sponge to wipe away the whole horizon? What did we do when we loosened this earth from its sun? (...) Whither do we move? Away from all suns? (...) Backwards, sideways, forwards, in all directions? Is there still an above and below? Do we not stray, as through infinite nothingness? Does not empty space breathe upon us? Has it not become colder? Does not night come on continually, darker and darker? Shall we not have to light lanterns in the morning?"[18]

Humanity's awareness of the death of God is an image of darkness, loss of orientation, and fading horizons. Barth's CD IV/3 can be read as a consciously told counter-story of light, finding paths, and horizons coming closer. Yet inside this counter-story, the hamartiological section (§ 70) serves as a counter-counter story, which resembles Nietzsche's original image.

The outline in this third section is a bit different here from the first two. The first two involved the upward and downward movement of sinful humanity over and against the downward and upward movement of Jesus the priestly God and royal man. The third volume is about the *outward* movement of God in Christ and through his Spirit, and presents Jesus as Victor by his prophetic witness who spreads light and conquers darkness by the word of the cross.[19] Seen from this perspective, sin is essentially an *inward* movement, which involves resisting the Holy Spirit.[20] Whereas God calls humanity to join God on God's mission, both church and world refuse to exist outwardly (*extra se*) and instead turn inward to their own systems. Humanity is not willing to submit to the prophetic witness of Christ as the son

---

18 F. W. Nietzsche, *The Gay Science* (1882, 1887), section 125.
19 Cf. Barth, *KD IV/3*, 7: "Die Versöhnung ist eben kein stummes, sondern ein lautes, kein dunkles, sondern ein helles und also kein in sich verschlossenes, sondern ein transeuntes, ein kommunikatives Geschehen. Sie wird nicht anders Ereignis, als indem sie sich selbst auch äußert, erschließt, mitteilt."
20 Cf. Matt Jenson, *The Gravity of Sin*, 155–81, showing how pride, sloth, and falsehood are in fact three instances of incurvation. Pride curves in because it cannot see in the other anything but a useful extension of itself; sloth curves in because a slothful person is unable to engage with the other as herself; falsehood evidently curves in because interrupting truth is blocked off. From here, Jenson renders a meaningful engagement between Barth and a feminist theology on sin.

of righteousness, but rather hides in darkness like a startled squid.[21] Falsehood, for Barth, is not about telling occasional lies but fundamentally entails replacing God's saving word of the cross with human systems, stories, and worldviews: "If pride and sloth are the act, then falsehood is the word of the man of sin. This obviously completes its basic character as a deflection, as a caricature of the threefold office and work of Jesus Christ."[22]

The word of the cross has five characteristics: 1) it is spoken from beyond the silence of death, i.e., by God; 2) it is about reconciliation; 3) which in turn has its mystery as the eternal decision of God to surrender Godself to uplift humanity; 4) which is something utterly strange to human understanding; 5) and can therefore only be heard truly through the power of the Holy Spirit.[23]

Over and against this, sin is the evasive movement to subdue and repress the truth of this word of the cross. Of course, the world plainly denies Christ to be Lord. But the church shares in the sin of falsehood just as much as the world, perhaps even more so. The inward movement simply takes a different form here, and Barth is most interested in this ecclesiastical way of sinning. The world of Jew and Greek openly distances itself at this point. But the church has found other ways to replace God's truth with falsehood, not by rejecting it, but much more subtly: by controlling and incorporating it into its own interests. The church has ways of "patronising, interpreting, domesticating, acclimatising, accommodating and quietly, but decisively and successfully correcting," as Barth puts it.[24] Whereas the word of the cross aims to restore God and humanity in mutual freedom and mutual love, the point of clerical systems is that they always tend to exclude freedom. As Barth writes, "Ultimately, everything that can and must be said about the people of sin in their encounter with Jesus Christ, the true witness, what frightens them and what they lie about, can and must be brought back to a common denominator: it is about freedom."[25] Freedom is unbearable for sinners. Rather than being freed from the human urge to be like God, humanity places God and human beings together in one single system. Rather than acknowledging the freedom of God's humble deed, humanity construe God as some "highest being." And rather than acknowledging humanity's own restored freedom, human beings construe themselves as dependent. Barth refers to the biblical

---

21 Barth, *KD IV/3*, 430; the metaphor is borrowed from Zwingli.
22 Barth, *KD IV/3*, 430.
23 Barth, *KD IV/3*, 470–86.
24 Barth, *KD IV/3*, 502.
25 Barth, *KD IV/3*, 514.

story about Hiob here: his friends knew all too well what God was doing, but they left both God and Hiob no room for freedom. According to Barth, truth is not like a coherent and closed system of accurate statements. Such a doctrinal system is at best a limited and fragmented reflection of truth. At worst, it is nothing but falsehood. Truth always comes with freedom.

In Barth's concluding section on being under sin, he labels the threat of the consequences of falsehood as nothing less than "damnation" (§ 70.3). He vividly describes here what happens when both church and world shut themselves off from God's truth in Christ. The sin of the world is that it does not believe in God's gracious, humble, and uplifting movement. But denying Christ as Lord does not mean one has no lord at all. In fact, people surrender themselves "to their own unworthy ideas" (Romans 1:28). They get to live in strange subjective realities, which no longer correspond to objective reality.[26] Barth must have been thinking of ideologies such as fascism, communism, and liberalism with their respective dogmas, but the list can be extended easily to other powers, worldviews, doctrinal systems, and conspiracy theories (cf. also the "lordless powers" Barth discusses in CD IV/4 on the Christian life). Surrendering to these kinds of religious or secular worldviews apart from Christ comes with fatal consequences. Untrue ideas and images begin to shape reality. Whoever goes along with it ends up in a bubble conditioned by absolute truths.In living in these bubbles, without Christ as the sun and spiritual center, people lose their orientation. Restlessly, humanity tries to find a fixed point where everything comes together, but this point cannot be found (*keine Mitte*). Without a center, there is also no real boundary (*keine Peripherie*). Small things can suddenly become very important. Mosquitoes become elephants, but camels are swallowed without a problem. Without a center and without boundaries, human beings flock back and forth, sometimes attracted to one thing and then to another. They merge into the masses or isolate individually, but they never arrive at real community (*kein Miteinander*), because no final stability can be found. Everything is open, but nothing can be truly finished (*keine Stetigkeit*). Each bubble brings its own linguistic field with specific areas where speech becomes vague, unclear, and ultimately deceitful. Truth becomes increasingly arbitrary. Doubt about the ability to distinguish fake from reality or from a fixed-point creeps in (*Problematik der menschlichen Sprache*). Barth manages to convey a feeling of horror here not unlike that of some dystopian novelists in seeing through

---

26   Barth, *KD IV/3*, 540–5.

the fabric of life in modern society. Nietzsche's parable of the madman is, for Barth, a dreadful truth: postmodernity's loss of orientation is what happens when human beings "loosen this earth from its sun," which for Barth is Christ, the Light of Life (§ 69.2).

4. Nothingness

Why do people do the things they do? Why do they sin? Often, very plausible explanations are provided for human actions. When accounting for one's actions, all kinds of causal links and rational reasons are brought to the surface. So much so that one often comes to the point of thinking that one could not have done otherwise: "I had to, there were no other options, it was necessary." But are human beings still free, then? And if not, how can one human being accuse another of sin? Does not the very concept of sin imply that human beings are free to choose otherwise?

According to Nietzsche, freedom and sin are connected concepts. Freedom of will was invented for the sake of burdening people with a conscience. Just as sin does not exist, so too this kind of freedom does not exist either. In *Twilight of the Idols*, Nietzsche writes, "Men were considered 'free' only so that they might be considered guilty – could be judged and punished: consequently, every act had to be considered as willed, and the origin of every act had to be considered as lying within the consciousness."[27] And in his *Beyond Good and Evil*, Nietzsche remarks:

> "The desire for 'freedom of will' in the superlative, metaphysical sense, such as still holds sway, unfortunately, in the minds of the half-educated, the desire to bear the entire and ultimate responsibility for one's actions oneself, and to absolve God, the world, ancestors, chance, and society therefrom, involves nothing less than to be precisely this *causa sui*, and, with more than Munchausen daring, to pull oneself up into existence by the hair, out of the slough of nothingness."[28]

Texts like these are doors to enormous fields of philosophical investigation, which cannot be unpacked here. But it does help to look at what has not been mentioned to this point: Barth's doctrine of sin is grounded in his doctrine of nothingness ("Das Nichtige," CD III/3). Alongside death, evil,

---

27 F. W. Nietzsche, *Twilight of the Idols* (1888), The Four Great Errors, part 7.
28 F. W. Nietzsche, *Beyond Good and Evil* (1886), part 20.

demons, lordless powers, and perhaps creaturely shadows, sin is the most prominent feature of nothingness. Sin is nothingness in action.

This does not only mean that sin is futile, nor that sin is only a mistake, although its nothingness means this too. This also does not mean, as some critics have objected, that sin seems to be something quite harmless for Barth. On the contrary, for Barth, sin is primarily a statement about the *gravity and origin* of sin.[29] What is sin? Where does sin come from? What is its cause? Why do people effectively deny Christ and live in pride, sloth, and falsehood?

Barth does not need a free will, but he does not succumb to Nietzsche's determinism either.[30] For Barth, the answer is straightforward: human beings sin for no reason. There is no explanation. Sin is simply a *brutum factum*. Barth stresses this point repeatedly in his discussion of stupidity as the first aspect of sloth:

> "Stupidity would not be what it is if it had a meaning and reason and could therefore be explained. The stupid, always untimely movements to the left and to the right in which it manifests itself are relatively explainable. How should they not all have their more or less plausible reasons and occasions, their internal and external motives and quietives, from which one can at least understand them to a good extent. But its root, the stupidity of stupidity, its sin manifested in its actions and omissions, is incomprehensible and inexplicable. It has no reason, as certainly as it comes directly from the void and consists in man's turning towards the void (*"Sie hat keinen Grund, so gewiss sie eben als solche direkt aus dem Nichtigen stammt und in des Menschen Zuwendung zum Nichtigen besteht"*). It is just a fact, *factum brutum*. All we can say about it is that he does it: he is free and makes no use of the fact that he is so; he is raised and lets himself fall; He is in the light and also has eyes to see it and yet does not see, so he remains in darkness; he hears and yet becomes no hearer, not obedient. Why? With what sense? For no reason, no sense! It's just that he's just doing it that way. Anyone who wanted to attribute a reason and meaning to this event would only show that they do not know that they are talking about evil, which is just evil."[31]

---

29 Cf. Wüthrich, *Gott und das Nichtige*, 181: "Eine Herabminderung der menschlichen Schuld und Verantwortlichkeit angesichts der Sünde ist damit nicht angezeigt. Im Gegenteil, das Nichtigkeitsurteil deklariert gerade die Absurdität und Unverzeihlichkeit der Sünde vor Gott."
30 Barth, *KD IV/1*, 458; Barth, *CD IV/2*, 558–64.
31 Barth, *KD IV/2*, 467–477.

The same is true of all other aspects of sin.³² There may be plausible reasons and occasions for sin, but in the end, sin has essentially no reason. Sin is groundless, and human explanations for sin only ever get half-way, but they never manage to fully account for human deeds. Human beings differ from Christ for no reason. Sin is irrational and without explanation. Like grace, sin is inexplicable. Sin and grace are both *sine ratione*, for no reason.

At this point, many questions come to the fore. The idea of something happening "without reason" is diametrically opposed to the axiom which became foundational for modernity, the "principle of ground" (*Satz vom Grund, nihil est sine ratione*), which posits that nothing is without grounding.³³ Of course, Barth does not mean that sinful acts are exempt from scientific scrutiny or that sinful acts happen accidentally or by chance. Sins are also acts that happen within a context. But for Barth, this context is never sufficient to account for sins completely, because sin is never rational. Christ would not have sinned in any context, thus sin is never necessary. Barth came close to Aristotle with his dual architecture that placed Christ in the middle, and Barth also seems to come close to Immanuel Kant with his understanding of evil as irrationality.³⁴ Rationality is following Christ, who is the ratio (*logos*) of God; sin is following the lead of nothingness, which darkens the human mind.

The only sufficient explanation for irrational fruits is an irrational tree, rooted in darkness and nothingness because the human being lives in falsehood, resisting the light of Christ. For such a tree, sin is necessary indeed. The human being cannot but bear sinful fruits and is in severe danger of being cut down and thrown into the fire of damnation. Sinful humanity is not a neutral *causa sui*, but in fact, humanity has lost its selfhood to nothingness.

---

32 Cf. for example Barth, *KD IV/1*, 466 (first aspect of pride): "Aber eben zu einer Begründung: woher und wozu wir diese hochmütigen Menschen sind, kann es dabei nicht kommen. Das Absurde, das wir tun, ist als solches unbegründet. Wir können es gerade nur zu beschreiben versuchen." Another example can be found in Barth, *KD IV/1*, 513 (second aspect): "Einen Grund dafür, dass er jenes nicht will und darum dieses wollen muss, gibt es nicht. Wir werden das Sein des Menschen auch nach dieser Bestimmung nur eben beschreiben können." Wüthrich, surprisingly, does not pay much attention to this aspect of nothingness, and seems to have missed how nothingness for Barth is the source of sin.

33 Cf. Martin Heidegger, *Der Satz vom Grund* (Pfullingen: Günther Neske, 1957).

34 Cf. I. Kant, *Grundlegung zur Metaphysik der Sitten* (1785); *Die Religion innerhalb der Grenzen der bloßen Vernunft* (1793/94); J. Rohls, "Kants Deutung des Sündenfalls," in *Religionsphilosophie nach Kant. Neue Horizonte der Religionsphilosophie*, ed. M. Kühnlein (Berlin: J.B. Metzler, 2023).

Nothingness is a power stronger than humanity, determining humanity to sin. Nothingness can only be overcome by the grace of God. For Barth, this has already been accomplished. Everything humanity says about sin would better be stated in the past perfect tense.[35] Pride, sloth, and falsehood are about humanity as it is not.

---

35 Barth, *KD IV/1*, 560.

Aku Stephen Antombikums

"The Judge Judged in Our Place"
Sin and Atonement in Karl Barth

Introduction

Recently, analytic theologians[1] have begun to reexamine traditional Christian doctrines using the methods of analytic philosophy and theology. Unlike analytic philosophy, analytic theology might be regarded as an insider's philosophical study of the Christian faith. In so doing, analytic theology does not question confessional Christianity; instead, in its ambitious and rigorous study, it seeks to present a precisely logical and viable understanding of the Christian faith. Such exercises have now been extended to issues that do not receive special attention from analytic philosophers. One of such topics is the doctrine of atonement. This paper is part of such an enterprise aimed at drawing lessons from Barth for the current discussion.

The doctrine of atonement as understood today has its origin in the Hebrew word כַּפָּרָה, which has been variously translated as expiation, ransom, to appease, to cover, forgiveness, satisfaction, reconciliation, and the like. The entirety of Judaism as a cultic religion is completely saturated with the notion of atonement. Bernard Low argues that "In fact, all of its principal offerings – the burnt offering, the grain offering, the well-being offering, the sin offering and the guilt offering – have an atoning function in addition to other functions."[2] In the Old Testament, atonement could be understood as

---

1 Speaking about the re-emergence of interest by analytic philosophers in the doctrine of atonement and other core Christian doctrines, William Craig argues that "So philosophers have been actively engaged in discussion of the doctrines of the Trinity, Incarnation, and Atonement, which might be called "the big three" of peculiarly Christian doctrines." "Philosophical Issues in the Atonement," in *T&T Clark Handbook of Analytic Theology*, ed. James M. Arcadi and James T. Turner, Jr (London: T&T Clark, 2021), 231–243, 231.
2 Bernard Law, "The Logic of Atonement in Israel's Cult," *Scripture and Interpretation* 3, no. 1 (2009): 5–32, 6.

appeasing the wrath of the divine by the worshipper who fails to live up to their theological obligations. This failure, a bridge of contract, or, in other words, sin, means that the worshipper who fails to meet their theological obligation or terms of the condition of the covenant as in the Suzerain-Vesal treaty will lose their right to protection. The only way to restore such a broken relationship with God was through atonement. There were several types of atonement in the Old Testament, which we do not need to mention here. The central idea of the Book of Leviticus with respect to the atonement is that the fall has a consequence for the descendants of Adam. Further, apart from their participation in the sin of Adam, the worshipers were, at the time, breaking the laws of God. Instead of facing the wrath of God, God graciously provides an escape route for the defaulter through the atonement.

The worshipper was requested to bring gifts to appease God's wrath. The writer of Hebrews (Hebrews 10) argues that those gifts, in other words, sacrifices, did not lead to the complete eradication of the errors of the worshippers. The errors were covered temporarily to be remembered on the day of atonement rather than wholly blotted out, as understood in the New Testament. This explains why the erring worshippers had to present themselves repeatedly at the Mercy Seat after presenting their sacrifices to receive temporary forgiveness for their sins. However, the New Testament presents a complete reversal of the futile exercise of the Old Testament. Bible writers, including contemporary Christian philosophers and theologians, argue that Christ was sacrificed once and for all, and therefore, believers no longer need to make further sacrifices for the forgiveness of their sins.

The question of the proper terminology for the work of Christ has received tremendous treatment from theologians since antiquity. As stated above, analytic theologians are also reminiscing about the nature of Christ's work on the cross. Discussing the atonement seems to raise a few challenges. The first reason for these struggles is simple: the Bible seems to provide various terminologies for Christ's work: ransom (Mark 10:45), substitution (Romans 3:21–31), satisfaction (Romans 3:25, 5:9), reconciliation (2 Corinthians 5:19), and the like. Secondly, contrary to other Christian doctrines, there has never been any unanimous agreement about the *name* and *mode* of how humanity got saved after the Fall.[3] As a result, theologians seem to concentrate on the notions of atonement as moral influence, ransom, pe-

---

3   Kirk Lougheed, *A Relational Theory of the Atonement: African Contributions to Western Philosophical Theology* (London: Routledge, 2024), 1.

nal substitution, and satisfaction theories, including *Christus Victor,* among others.

The ransom theory of the atonement traces its roots back to Origen. This theory is undoubtedly contingent on Jesus' statement in Mark 10:45: "The Son of Man did not come to be served but to give himself as a ramson for sinners" (paraphrased). Paul's statement in 1 Corinthians 6:20 that believers were bought with a price seems to align with Christ's statement. As a result, theologians argued that when Adam and Eve disobeyed God, they handed over their authority and freedom to the devil, although they belonged to God. Getting God's possession back in a judicial context demands that there must be a price – in other words, a ransom – to reclaim humanity, and therefore, the Son of God came to offer Himself as a ransom. Justice was done when Christ died on the cross, but the dead could not hold Him.[4] However, who received the price or the ramson is another subject of debate. Anselm, in his satisfaction theory, rejected that there was any payment of ransom.

Having rejected the ransom theory of atonement, Anselm presented a satisfaction theory.[5] He argued that the ransom theory is logically flawed, especially the notion that ransom was paid to the devil. If it is conceded that the devil is God's rebellious creature, then God and humanity owe the devil no payment because humans' sin was not a rebellion against the devil but against God.[6] In a dialogical manner, Anselm and Boso extrapolate the satisfaction theory of the atonement from divine justice, the enormity of sin, and the mercy and compassion of God.

Boso seems to argue that God should have used other means to save humanity without causing the Son of God to suffer on the cross. He stated, "If you say that God, who, as you believe, created the universe by a word, could not do all these things by a simple command, you contradict yourselves, for you make him powerless. Or, if you grant that he could have done these things in some other way, but did not wish to, how can you vindicate

---

[4] Joshua C Thurow, "Atonement," *The Stanford Encyclopedia of Philosophy,* ed. Edward N. Zalta and Uri Nodelman (2023). https://plato.stanford.edu/archives/sum2023/entries/atonement/>.

[5] See Eleanor Stump, *Atonement: Oxford Studies in Analytic Theology* (Oxford: Oxford University Press, 2018).

[6] Anselm of Canterbury, *Proslogium; Monologium; An Appendix in Behalf of the Fool by Gaunilon; and Cur Deus Homo,* trans. from Latin by Sidney Norton Deane (Downers Grove: The Open Court, 1923) 1:7, 187–188.

his wisdom, when you assert that he desired, without any reason, to suffer things so unbecoming?"[7]

Anselm's argument presented three fundamental responses to Boso. First, due to the creator-creature relationship, humans are obligated to honour God. However, what happened in the Garden of Eden was a dishonour to the glory of God. "Therefore to sin is nothing else than not to render to God his due."[8] This dishonour in a judicial context demands that humans be punished to satisfy justice. This might not necessarily be to satisfy the wrath of God but to satisfy justice, as long as God is just yet a merciful God.

Second, Anselm argues that the suffering of the Son of God on the cross was not imposed on Him, but He willingly, in obedience to the Father, took that path to satisfy justice.[9] In the third place, what has been stolen must be restored. When humanity dishonours God and robs Him of His glory, it must be restored. Nothing passes by in God's kingdom without being discharged; therefore, sin cannot be cancelled without compensation. If that were to be the case, there would be no distinction between the guilty and the innocent. After all, it is an injustice to cancel sin only by compassion.[10] Although the conclusion in this paragraph seems as if God could lose His glory given human disobedience, I doubt Anselm really meant that, or that is the case here. If that is the case, this will be contrary to common sense because the Godhead cannot lose any of His great-making properties, including His glory. What I think is at stake is that every action has a corresponding consequence. However, given God's righteousness, humans in their fallen state could not satisfy the righteous demands of the righteous laws of God. Therefore, it costs God His Son through whom He was reconciling humanity to Himself after satisfying the demands of the law.

The moral influence theory sees Christ as a prototype for believers in Christ to emulate His moral character, while penal substitution originated in the thoughts of Luther and Calvin. Contrary to the ransom theory and close to the satisfaction theory, the penal substation theory posits that Christ took our punishment. This substitution led to the satisfaction of the justice of God while reconciling humans to God. This view has met a few objections, especially the fact that the substitute is not eternally condemned but living. Lastly, Christus Victor, although developed by Gustaf Aulen, has Luther as

---

7   Anselm, *Cur Deus Homo*, 1:6, 186.
8   Anselm, *Cur Deus Homo*, 1:10, 198–201.
9   Anselm, *Cur Deus Homo*, 1:9 193–197.
10 Anselm, *Cur Deus Homo*, 1:12, 204–206.

its chief precursor. It centres on the notion that humans were enslaved by the devil. However, Christ's death and resurrection conquered the enemy and freed the captives. Through this victory, humans have been liberated from the bondage of the devil, sin, and death.[11]

The emphasis of these theories of atonement, as mentioned above, is on the consequences of the decision of our first parents in the Garden of Eden. Participation in that disobedience made us enemies of God either as a result of justice or because we failed to love God and chose our path, and in the end, became slaves of the devil. However, God, in His justice, mercy, love, and compassion, gave up His only Son, who, in His incarnation, obedience in suffering, death, and resurrection, reconciled us to the Father. Sin, justice, and mercy are the nuclei of the aforementioned theories. As we have shown below, this does not seem to be the case with Barth. Now, let us turn to Barth.

Das Nichtige

As mentioned above, sin – a break in a relationship – is the basis for the need for atonement. In Christianity, sin has been traditionally understood as something inherent to humanity, beginning with the decision of Adam and Eve, who disobeyed God despite being created without it. So, sin is understood as humanity turning away from its maker. Since Adam (the red clay in the Hebrew language) became a living being after God breathed into its nostrils, the consequence of sin is technically the unmaking of such living breath. As a result, together with our first parent, after participating in such disobedience that led to the pollution and corruption of the *ruach* and the *imago Dei* in us, we were becoming unbecoming and gradually returning to the dust where we came from. To unmake our unbecoming, theologians extrapolating from Genesis 3 argue that only God could restore us to Himself given that we could not help ourselves nor could we restore the broken relationship with God.

---

11 Thurow, "Atonement," *The Stanford Encyclopedia of Philosophy*. https://plato.stanford.edu/archives/sum2023/entries/atonement/>

Similar to Augustine,[12] Barth refers to sin as *das Nichtige,* which is translated as *nothingness.*[13] He argues that "evil is a form of that nothingness which as such is absolutely subject to God."[14] Barth warns that we should not take evil seriously because 'God is its Lord.' Sin is neither *original* nor independent of God nor a counter-deity to God. Evil and nothingness seem to assume a *theodicean* role in Barth's thought. As its Lord, God might use it to accomplish His will.[15] On the cross, evil appeared to have a counter-power to God when Christ died. However, it was a mere deception. Evil believed the lie that it could take the life of God. Such a lie was overcome once and for all when Christ rose from death.[16]

I find two things interesting to reiterate here. First, the idea of the *originality* of sin seems not to point to the notion of original sin as traditionally understood in Christian theology.[17] Secondly, the issue of the *lie* evil believed about the Son of God comes closer to Origen's fish-hook-and-bait idea, including the purported deception God exemplified when He offered Christ to the devil. Although there seems to be such an idea in the back of Barth's mind while presenting this argument, I doubt this is what he intended to say. What is evident is the fact that on the cross and in the death of Christ, which is foolishness to the Gentiles but the power of God to believers, if Christ had not risen from death, evil would have triumphed over the second Person of

---

12 Augustine refers to evil as *privatio boni*, the privation of the Good. Augustine argues that "Everything that exists is good, then; and so evil, the source of which I was seeking, cannot be a substance, because if it were, it would be good." See Mark Scott, *Pathways in Theodicy: An Introduction to the Problem of Evil* (Minneapolis: Fortress, 2015), 84. cf. Augustine, St., *Confessions: The Nicene and Post Nicene Fathers*, ed. P. Schaff (Grand Rapids: Eerdmans, 1979) V.20, VII.12.18, VII.13.19.
13 See Shao Kai Tseng, *Barth's Ontology of Sin and Grace Variations on a Theme of Augustine* (London: Routledge, 2019).
14 Karl Barth, *Die Kirchliche Dogmatik IV/1: Die Lehre von der Versöhnung,* translated *Church Dogmatics IV/1: The Doctrine Of Reconciliation*, ed. G. W. Bromiley and T. F. Torrance (London: T&T Clark, 1956), §60: 406.
15 See Deborah Caswell, "Nothingness and the Left Hand of God: Evil, Anfechtung, and the Hidden God in Luther, Barth, and Jüngel," *Neue Zeitschrift für Systematische Theologie und Religionsphilosophie*, 64, no. 1 (2022): 24–49. https://doi.org/10.1515/nzsth-2022-0002
16 Barth, *CD IV/1*, §60: 406.
17 See Paul L. Allen, "Sin and Natural Theology: An Augustinian Framework Beyond Barth," *Neue Zeitschrift für Systematische Theologie und Religionsphilosophie*, 57, no. 1 (2015): 14–31. https://doi.org/10.1515/nzsth-2015-0002.

the Trinity and ultimately over God. However, this is not the case. God broke the power of evil once and for all in Christ at Golgotha.[18]

Contrary to the idea that humans were created free and therefore could possibly sin, which explains what happens in the Garden of Eden, Barth argues that it is erroneous to argue that man was a created a free creature to both obey and disobey God and therefore has the *possibility* to disobey God. Instead, the freedom to sin is not inherent in man from creation. It originated in him when he listened to the voice of the devil. As far as Barth is concerned, sin is an impossible possibility. It was an absurd event that had no origin external to man, nor was it part of a divine plan contrary to infralapsarianism.[19]

Sin, according to Barth, is expressly demonstrated in three ways: pride (CD IV/§60.2), sloth (CD IV/§65.2), and falsehood (CD IV/§70.2). Contrary to the conditions, limitations, and parameters set by God for Adam and Eve in the Garden, they listened to the voice of the devil and acted in arrogance against God's command. As is the case with Adam and Eve, Christians today are trying so hard to become like God, even though Christ became man out of humility. Barth argues that "Sin, therefore, in its totality is pride."[20] Pride, which is the actual sin, is believing in ourselves instead of Christ.[21] Unbelief in Christ and trying to be lords, although ontologically we cannot become God, but God can become man, is pride and a fruitless effort. In doing that, we try to be lords instead of servants, as Christ did. It is stated that *the Word became flesh* because God is God and is free to be anything He wants to be. But as humans, we cannot decide what we want to be. Man's attempt at becoming like God is the revelation of his impotence. However, God becoming flesh is the revelation of His divinity.[22]

Another way sin is expressed in humans is sloth (CD IV/§65.2). Through it, the human essence is diminished, we become stupid and cannot listen to God, we are inhuman in our dealings with fellow humans, we are afraid, and there is a separation between our minds and our bodies. Contrary to the aforementioned, Christ is always attentive to the Father; although He had two natures, He had only one essence, and He always and never feared anything. Lastly, sin expresses itself in us through falsehood. From the foregoing, we can see that Barth's understanding of sin as das Nichtige, which begets evil,

---

18 Barth, *CD IV/1*, §60: 407.
19 Barth, *CD IV/1*, §60: 408.
20 Barth, *CD IV/1*, §60: 413.
21 Barth, *CD IV/1*, §60: 414–415.
22 Barth, *CD IV/1*, §60: 417.

seems to be a different understanding of sin. Due to this understanding of sin, Barth's doctrine of atonement does not emphasise sin as the precondition for the incarnation and atonement. Instead, the revelation of the Son of God and His solidarity with sinners is the focus of Barth's explication of the atonement. This shift of attention does two things in the estimation of the current studies.

First, in this conception, the devil and the law, which reveal sin, lose their place of pride as the basis for the atonement. Secondly, the revelation of the divinity of Christ and His humility, humans' impotence, and the need to emulate Christ's humility are not only viable but also logically biblical. However, Barth's notion of sin as das Nichtige raises a few questions and objections, which I will mention toward the end of this paper. In what follows, I will examine why the Judge needed to be judged in our place, what this judgement meant for sinners, and what implications are there of this singular act on the sinners' past and present experiences in Christ.

1) Why was it necessary for the judge to be judged in our place?

As seen above, the weight of human sins and the love of God have always been at the centre of the doctrine of atonement. Anselm's conversation with Bosso, as cited above, and the necessity of satisfying the requirement of the law, which is a form of appeasement to atone for the wrath of an angry Judge, seems to be the order of the discussions. Either a price or ramson is paid (ransom theory), or the demand of the law is satisfied (satisfaction theory), Christ took the place of sinners through substitutions, or Christ triumphantly overcame the enemy of humanity. Amidst these, God's grace, love, and mercy are emphasised as the driving forces that cause God to become man for man's salvation. Contrary to the foregoing, Barth, in extrapolating why the Judge who knew no sin was judged for humankind, argues that such a judgement was a revelation of the second Person of the Trinity. Barth argues that the idea that in the atonement, the wrath of God was satisfied so that we do not need to suffer the consequences of our sins, as championed by Anselm, is strange to the New Testament. He argues that the emphasis should be on the fact that Christ, in His Person, has brought an end to us as sinners and, therefore, He cancelled sin. Not that He suffered our punishment, but He overcame sin.[23]

---

23 Barth, *CD IV/1*, §59: 253.

As with other traditional doctrines of atonement, Barth mentioned that the Judge did what we couldn't do for ourselves.[24] The severity of the human condition demands that only God-man can overcome it. "The very heart of the atonement is the overcoming of sin: sin in its character as the rebellion of man against God, and in its character as the ground of man's hopeless destiny in death. It was to fulfil this judgment on sin that the Son of God as man took our place as sinners."[25] However, the central issue, according to Barth, is not about the human condition but the nature of God. The passion of Christ on the cross was first a divine revelation of the Godhead before His identification with sinners. It is in the revelation of God's nature that the sinners, as a consequence, are acquitted and reconciled with the Father.[26] In the incarnation of the Lord, Barth argues that God became "[H]is own Doppelgänger."[27]

Speaking on Barth's understanding of divine revelation, Matthew J. A. Bruce argues that Barth is hesitant about the human faculty's ability to comprehend divine revelation in nature because they are part of the creation, and their knowledge is limited to what is within the creation. Therefore, as in the traditional understanding of divine revelation, Barth holds that God is self-revealing, and until He does so, no one human can understand Him. Bruce went on to argue that "The person of Jesus Christ is the definitive locus of God's self-revelation"[28] This is true because the atonement, according to Barth, is a special revealed history. It is the history of God's dealings with humanity. It is not only a special history of God and humanity but also a history of humanity.[29]

One may ask, what difference does distinguishing between God's special history and human history make? To me, the difference is that the atonement means a different thing to God and another to humanity. On the one hand, in this extraordinary history, God reveals Himself as being able to become human. It reveals the nature of the second Person of the Trinity. Contrary to this, on the other hand, it reveals humans' impotence and God's act of recon-

---

24 Barth, *CD IV/1*, §59: 211–212.
25 Barth, *CD IV/1*, §59: 253.
26 Barth, *CD IV/1*, §59: 212.
27 Alexander Garton-Eisenacher, *Divine Freedom and Revelation in Christ: The Doctrine of Eternity with Special Reference to the Theology of Karl Barth* (Göttingen: Vandenhoeck & Ruprecht, 2023), 25.
28 Mathew J. A. Bruce, "Barth on Revelation," in *The Wiley Blackwell Companion to Karl Barth: Barth and Dogmatics*, Volume I, First Edition, ed. George Hunsinger and Keith L. Johnson (New Jersey: Wiley Blackwell, 2020), 59–69, 66.
29 Barth, *CD IV/1*, §59: 171–172.

ciling sinful humans to God through the God-man. One fundamental difference we need to point out here is the fact that although God could become human, humans cannot become God. Barth argues that "The atonement is, noetically, the history about Jesus Christ, and ontically, Jesus Christ's own history. To say atonement is to say Jesus Christ. To speak of it is to speak of His history."[30] This history consists of the fact that humanity is guilty and condemned. However, God Himself took the initiative to reconcile humanity with God. God is Himself, both the reconciler and the reconciled, because He is both God and human. "It is in His self-offering to death that God has again found man and man God."[31]

Contrary to the Gentiles, who contemplate the incarnation of the Son as foolishness and not only against the rule of logic but practically impossible, Barth argues that although it seems paradoxical and contradictory, the incarnation, the journey of the Son into a distant land that appears to strip away His divinity, is the revelation of the Godhead. So, like with Jesus' statement to Philip, anyone who sees me has seen the Father, Barth argues, as traditionally upheld in Christian theology, that Christ is the climax of the revelation because "...in Christ, all the fullness of the Deity lives in bodily form" (Col. 2:9). What it means to be God or divine, Barth argues, is something we have to learn through divine revelation. However, "[I]f He has revealed Himself in Jesus Christ as the God who does this, it is not for us to be wiser than He and to say that it is in contradiction with the divine essence."[32] In other words, the coming of the Son of God in the form of man, His apparent fragility and incongruity with the nature of God as traditionally conceived in the Old Testament, is a further revelation of God-man. Therefore, this revelation is sufficient, and we do not need to look elsewhere, as seen in Colossians above.

2) What does this judgment mean for sinners?

Although Barth's view of the atonement does not align with the traditional doctrines of the atonement mentioned above, Adam J. Johnson argues that his treatment of the atonement is replete with substitutional and representa-

---

30 Barth, *CD IV/1*, §59: 172.
31 Barth, *CD IV/1*, §59: 172.
32 Barth, *CD IV/1*, §59: 186.

tional notions of the atonement.[33] This is true with respect to Barth's argument about the passion of Christ, as shown below.

First, this judgement means *Deus pro nobis*. Being judged in the sinners' place means God is for us and has not abandoned the world despite its sins. Barth argues that humans do not deserve any atonement and cannot save themselves.[34] Further, the fact that "Jesus Christ judges in our place means an immeasurable liberation and hope. The loss which we always bewail and which we seem to suffer means in reality that a heavy and indeed oppressive burden is lifted from us when Jesus Christ becomes our Judge."[35]

Barth argues that humanity by nature depends on Christ as an elder brother, but a brother from whom humanity cannot detach itself. Humanity's existence is through the grace of God. As the apostle Paul puts it, what is by grace is a gift, and the receiver has nothing to boast about because it is not based on merit. As the Judge, whatever Christ describes as righteous stands that way, and whatever He tags unrighteous is unrighteous. This explains why the revelations of His divinity and His willingness to take up our place made Him the sinful man before God and, conversely, rendered humanity upright before God. He judges from a *place* where no man can stand.[36] This 'place' seems to refer to the place of righteousness. However, Barth's reference to Jesus' starting from the vantage of preaching repentance for the coming kingdom seems to suggest that this *place* is not only a place of righteousness but the judgement throne at the eschaton.[37] Therefore, having demonstrated His impartial judgement to the extent that the Judge was condemned for identifying with His brothers, there can be no escape route for sinners except under the declaration of the Judge of all.

Although humanity sinned against God in the Garden of Eden, the understanding of this sin is not made glaring in humanity but in Christ. "It is again Jesus Christ in whose existence sin is revealed, not only in its actuality and sinfulness, but as the truth of all human being and activity."[38] It is fascinating to see how Barth seems to refer to Paul's argument in Galatians that the law reveals sin. Barth is here drawing a similarity between Christ, the

---

33 See Adam J. Johnson, "Barth on the Atonement," in *The Wiley Blackwell Companion to Karl Barth*, 147–158.
34 Barth, *CD IV/1*, §60: 397.
35 Barth, *CD IV/1*, §59: 233.
36 Barth, *CD IV/1*, §60: 400.
37 Barth, *CD IV/1*, §60: 399.
38 Barth, *CD IV/1*, §60: 401.

Judge and the enforcer of the law and the law. Christ is both revealing sin and, at the same time, the sinner who stands condemned by the law.

Further, just as the atonement is a revelation of Christ's divinity and humanity, it is also a revelation of the destructive power of sin. However, Barth quickly points out the distinction between how Christ reveals sin and how sin might be manifested in humanity. Of course, there is the tendency to see sin as a product of manipulation by a higher force and, therefore, to argue that humanity acted based on external influence. However, Barth insists that there is no distinction between the sinner and their sins. As seen above in his concept of das Nichtige, he argues that sin does exist on its own without the one committing it. Also, there are no classes or grades of sin, including conscious and unconscious sins. Each is the same. The distinction between lesser and greater sins and intentional and unintentional sins, for instance, the tax collectors versus the Pharisees, has always led to the separation of humans into the camp of more serious and less serious sinners. Contrarily, Barth argues that sin is sin. Christ eradicated the foregoing distinction when He declared Himself sinful in solidarity with sinners. In doing that, He identified not only with better sinners but with every sinner. After Jesus took up our sins, Barth argues that "When He bears it [our sins], even the greatest of sins cannot damn a man."[39]

Sin is indeed sin. However, it seems that a terrorist, a child abuser, or a narcist might be considered a terrible sinner before the law rather than a fornicator or an adulterer. If every sinful or erroneous action is taken to be the same, we may run into trouble regarding accountability before the law; after all, everyone is a sinner and, therefore, is not qualified to call other sinners out except Christ.

In Christ, the revelation of sin is not an actual action of the Judge but the actual condition and activity of all humanity. Human nature is altered in it, and humans are no longer themselves. Despite this alteration due to sin, Barth argues that humanity remains the excellent creature of God as it was in the beginning. This explains why, despite taking our place, the Judge was restored. Therefore, it follows that since the Judge who was not sinful took our place, borne our sin, and was not destroyed or His divinity lost, through Him, the image of God in us that was altered through sin is restored.[40]

---

[39] Barth, *CD IV/1*, §60: 401–403.
[40] Barth, *CD IV/1*, §60: 401, 404.

Secondly, this judgement means the salvation of humanity. Traditionally, there is no dispute concerning the benefit of Christ's death on the cross. Of course, as mentioned above, the various doctrines of the atonement used various terminologies for Christ's work and the manner through which such work was done. However, the result is the salvation of humankind. This is precisely what Barth also holds. As shown above, the atonement is Christ's history and human history, stating what He accomplished and what humans benefited from this accomplishment. This accomplishment concerns the fact that God in Christ saw humans' precarious condition and the need for salvation. The Son of God, the Judge, all in His compassion and willingness to identify with sinful humanity, went to a distant land where He seemed to be denuded of all His glories so that humans could be saved and reconciled with God. Therefore, "*Deus pro nobis* means that God in Jesus Christ has taken our place when we become sinners, when we become His enemies, when we stand as such under His accusation and curse, and bring upon ourselves our own destruction."[41]

Thirdly, this judgement leads to union with Christ. Christians are not only saved graciously without merit, but the prime benefit of their salvation is union with Christ. Christ took our place, all the punishments we were due to receive; He took everything on our behalf.[42] Not only that, He brought us into unity with the triune God. In the event of the atonement, Barth argues that "[…] God allows the world and humanity to take part in the history of the inner life of His Godhead, in the movement in which from and to all eternity He is Father, Son and Holy Spirit, and therefore the one true God."[43] This union with Christ has several implications for the Christian life, as mentioned below.

Fourthly, this judgement reveals Christ's virtue of humility and its implications for Christians. God the Son condescends Himself for the sake of humanity. Robert B. Price argues that "If Barth were to rewrite his doctrine of the divine perfections (CD II/1), he would not add humility to the list. But he would ensure that 'all the predicates of [the] Godhead' were 'filled out and interpreted' more fully in the light of the Son's humility."[44] Barth calls this condescension "the aspect of the grace of God in Jesus Christ in which

---

41 Barth, *CD IV/1*, § 59: 216.
42 Barth, *CD IV/1*, §59: 215–216.
43 Barth, *CD IV/1*, §59: 215.
44 Robert B. Price, "Barth on the Incarnation" in *The Wiley Blackwell Companion to Karl Barth*, 137–145, 141.

it comes to man as the (sinful) creature of God freely, without any merit or deserving, and therefore from outside, from above – which is to say, from God's standpoint, the aspect of His grace in which He does something unnecessary and extravagant, binding and limiting and compromising and offering Himself in relation to man by having dealings with him and making Himself his God. In the fact that God is gracious to man, all the limitations of man are God's limitations, all his weaknesses, and more, all his perversities are His."[45] He associates with fallen humans, unlike the priest and the Levite in the parable of the Good Samaritan.

3) What are the implications of this singular act on the sinners' past and present experiences in Christ?

In the atonement, Christ became both our substitute and representative. Marco Hofheinz argues that according to Barth, the Christian life is not lived in a vacuum but in Christ through baptism. The Christian life is a life of zeal and passion. He argues that Barth sees the Christian life as "To take part in the uprising against the disorder of the world; To oppose the Lordless powers; To join in the coming kingdom of God; To work for the human justice, freedom, and peace that reflects the justice, freedom, and peace of God's coming kingdom."[46] If this is the case, it follows that the Christian life cannot be free from suffering, especially in the form of persecution.

Barth argues that the doctrine of atonement differentiates the Almighty God from other gods because they are unwilling and incapable of doing what He did in Christ on the cross. Further, it expresses the humility of the Son of God. The Synoptic Gospels present Christ as both a Lord and a suffering servant who is obedient to the will of the Father. The will of the Father on earth is the redemption of humankind as it is done in heaven, even though this will not serve Christ's purpose. "He emptied Himself and took the form of a servant" (Phil. 2:7); "He humbled Himself, and became obedient unto death, even the death of the cross" (Phil. 2:8). In other words: "He who was rich became poor" (2 Cor. 8:9).[47] He was cursed for us and made flesh: Barth

---

45 Barth, *CD IV/1*, §59: 158, 282.
46 Marco Hofheinz, "Barth on the Christian Life," in *The Wiley Blackwell Companion to Karl Barth*, 355–367, 366.
47 Barth, *CD IV/1*, §59: 156.

argues that to be made flesh refers to His relationship with humanity as a result of being under the wrath of God and in a state of perishing.[48]

Barth argues that Christ's passion, as presented in the New Testament with its ethics, compels us to see a distinction between the followers of Christ and those who are not. Believers must imitate God, as in Eph 5, and be perfect as their Father in Heaven, as in Matthew 5.[49] From this point, they cannot choose whether they will exalt or abase themselves, whether they will save their life or lose it and in that way save it, whether they will leave or take up their cross, whether they will be offended by the beatitudes or put themselves under the light of them, whether they will hate their enemies or love them, whether they will accept or not accept the exhortation to ὑποταγή, to ὑπακοή, to τιμή, to the bearing of the burdens of others, to suffering in the discipleship of Christ."[50]

The New Testament ethics emphasise the importance of obedience, submission, and humility in discipleship. It implies that fulfilling the need for obedience rests on the God whose name and authority it is expected of, in contrast to the scribes and Pharisees who tie heavy burdens on their followers without using their fingers to move them. If God were like these, the morality of the New Testament may have been arbitrary, facultative and incidental, resulting in a system of morality that extols its idealism or impatience. The New Testament contends, however, that this ethics reflects God's divine character and that He does not exist above it. This ethics is not a moral code but reflects who He is.[51] In other words, Christ kept an ethical standard for all Christians to follow, especially when He said, take up your cross and follow me. Barth argues that God's true divinity is revealed through Christ's humility, which can be confirmed through our humiliation. This humility is a novum mysterium, demonstrating His love and life even in death. It is a fundamental aspect of God's being, and understanding Christ's deity and suffering is crucial for understanding the free love of God in the atonement.[52]

In His agony, the Judge was in solidarity with sinners. He is a perfect sacrifice for us, once and for all. As stated above, God did for us in Jesus what we could not do for ourselves. In doing so, He reveals His glory so that humans may have reason to praise Him, although He does not need their

---

48 Barth, *CD IV/1*, §59: 171.
49 Barth, *CD IV/1*, §59: 190.
50 Barth, *CD IV/1*, §59: 191.
51 Barth, *CD IV/1*, §59: 190–191.
52 Barth *CD IV/1*, §59: 192–193.

praise because He is contented in Himself.[53] This passion is the radical divine action that destroys the primary evil in the world, bringing in a new man and establishing a new world. It is the divine action of atonement that has taken place for us.[54] Faith in God's Word, specifically in Jesus Christ, is the only way to overcome the idea of an impatient God. God's patience is not only adequate towards us but also in judgment and punishment. By believing in God's Word, we can accept His patience and the possibility and reality of it. The only way to show gratitude for our lives is through faith in Jesus Christ and to love our neighbours as ourselves. The relationship with Jesus Christ allows us to endure suffering and the gift of our life for good, even in the face of inevitable death. This faith in God's Word allows us to grasp the promise of eternal life and the glory that will be revealed in us.[55]

Conclusion

Barth's view of sin and atonement differs significantly from the traditional views. This significant shift has enhanced our understanding of the atonement from the perspective of the revelation of the Son of God and the triune God. The atonement is also a revelation of sin on the one hand as pride, sloth, and falsehood and as das Nichtige on the other. This understanding has a theodicean motif, and as a result of it, the emphasis of the atonement in Barth is not about satisfying divine justice due to the sin of our first parents. However, the nucleus of the discussion is God the Son, whose atoning work on the cross in our place is not as traditionally understood, but in overcoming sin, we are saved, reconciled to God, united with the Trinity, and therefore also share in the passion of Christ.

---

53 Barth, *CD IV/1*, §59: 211–212.
54 Barth, *CD IV/1*, §59: 247.
55 Barth, *CD IV/1*, §60: 412.

Jared Stacy

Agents of Reconciliation Amidst the Anthropocene

The Offer of Barth For The Church Facing Climate Crisis

Introduction

A common practice in the present day is to reference the crisis of climate change as a "climate apocalypse."[1] This read of climate change often refers the crisis to extinction scenarios with attending extinction activisms conditioned by technocratic teleologies and risk management programs.[2] Such a discursive operation highlights the need for theological accounts of the climate crisis to contend with this refracted, doomsday reception of "apocalypse" and its continued association with Christian theology.

Protestant theology must retrieve and revive the essential Christological discipline of the apocalyptic amidst popular references to "apocalypse" and in this case "climate apocalypse." This retrieval occurs by way of a reorientation prefigured in the primal recognition that doomsday scenarios of are not synonymous with understandings of the apocalyptic in Christian theology and ethics.

The most rudimentary etymological gloss of "apocalypse" indicates a sort of disclosure. Pressed into service of the Church's witness, a decidedly Christian apocalyptic is rooted in and proceeds from the revelatory event of Jesus Christ. As Nancy Duff observes, such a story

---

[1] Chris Methmann and Delf Rothe, "Politics for the Day after Tomorrow: The Logic of Apocalypse in Global Climate Politics," *Security Dialogue* 43, no. 4 (August 1, 2012): 323–44, 323.

[2] Methmann and Rothe, "Politics for the Day after Tomorrow," 323–324.

"is concerned not with the future end of the world, but with God's in-breaking in Jesus Christ – an in-breaking that defeats the powers and principalities that hold the world in bondage."[3]

In contrast, apocalypse-as-doomsday imagines an event unmoored from the Christian story, without reference to the salvation of Christ and his expansive rule over the cosmos. Notably, Christian apocalypse is not triumphantly realized in this respect, but limited and awaiting fulfillment. Barth puts it well,

> "even the presence of Jesus in the Spirit, for all its fullness, can only be a pledge or first installment of what awaits the community as well as the whole universe."[4]

This limited aspect of a decidedly Christian apocalyptic raises the question of how the church-community conceives of its present time, even one marked by climate change. Hans Ulrich notes Barth rejects the notion of an "empty, indeterminate saeculum."[5] In Barth's refusal, Ulrich conceives of a Messianic-Apocalyptic which links the decisive event of Christ to the church-community in present, fragmentary time.[6] Christian ethics according to such a Messianic-Apocalyptic,

> "is in essence concerned with the Christian ethos as a lived witnessing to God's present working to initiate and realize God's new reality in determinate places, with determinate people."[7]

Before the church-community encounters the activisms of a "climate apocalypse", its first encounter is with the living God who constitutes and sustains the church according to the apocalyptic revelation of Christ. In this renewing encounter through practices of worship and sacrament, the witness and presence of the church-community finds itself with both a critical and constructive presence in the political arena full of climate apocalypse and

---

3   Nancy J. Duff, "Apocalyptic Ethics, End-Time Christians, and the Storming of the US Capitol," *Studies in Christian Ethics* 34, no. 4 (November 2021): 467–81, 470–1.
4   Barth, *CD III/2*, Study Version, 468.
5   Hans Günter Ulrich, *Transfigured Not Conformed: Christian Ethics in a Hermeneutic Key*, ed. Brian Brock, T&T Clark Enquiries in Theological Ethics (London / New York: Bloomsbury Academic, 2021),71.
6   "Christians are challenged to live within the apocalyptic story in a Messianic way, in a Messianic time – meaning that the apocalypse is not just the judgment of this aion, but has its very own positive appearance and determined reality in personal experience." Ulrich, *Transfigured Not Conformed,* 66-70.
7   Ibid., 70.

activisms. These preliminary moves showcase the way in which apocalyptic theology arrests the church-community's unrestricted use of "apocalypse" as the common way to frame climate change by doomsday, extinction scenarios. The church-community cannot conceive of its responsibility amidst "climate apocalypse" without reflection on what it means to be determined by the apocalypse of Christ expressed in a living out of its Christian ethos.

These locating remarks on the Christian apocalypse serve to frame a cursory examination of the offer of Barth's project for the church in the West facing the reality of climate crisis. Within the architecture of *Church Dogmatics*, where both sin and guilt are illumined in the apocalypse of Christ, the church-community finds grounds for its witness amidst a torrent of varying political activisms which trade on "apocalypse" to depict urgency. On this basis, this article suggests a way in which Barth's doctrines of election, creation, and reconciliation can be read to form a constellation which resources the church in the West as it confronts climate change. It does this by disciplining its speech and action according to Christ in an apocalyptic key.

On the Guilt of the Post-Christian West

By first answering claims of "climate apocalypse" with the Christian apocalypse I suggest the church-community begins to recapture its distinctive identity as an agent of reconciliation in a thicker and more concrete way.

Now we turn to ask in what way might this apocalyptic determination and disposition might generate a lived response from the church-community. The witness to God's reconciliation amidst activisms of extinction empties the power of climate apocalypse slogans while raising the question of human solidarity and responsibility in view of climate devastation. In this sense, being determined by the apocalyptic of Christian theology is not grounds for denying responsibility to address the material conditions and guilt of climate change. The church-community determined by Christ is in no position to deny this material devastation and justify itself in view of its guilt in sacralizing the economic and industrial practices of the West.

The material facts which attend the climate crisis as understood by prevailing scientific and scholarly consensus can be said to emerge from one primary meta-fact, the Anthropocene. The Anthropocene refers to an entire geological epoch of time characterized by human beings as the preeminent and dominant natural force.[8] This is both chronic and acute. Studies show that humankind, since the end of the first millennium AD, moves more sediment than all natural processes combined.[9] At the current rate, humanity could collectively fill the Grand Canyon in 50 years.[10] These and other material facts which recount the impact of humanity on natural processes define the dimensions of the Anthropocene.

The material content of these facts can be read theologically as provisional, refracted, or immediate fragments of collective and shared guilt. These fragmentary facts however are not the basis for theological reflection on and narration of the climate crisis. They are, in an immediate sense, part of a common lexicon, useful in the political for speaking about the climate crisis and coordinating united activisms in post-Christian societies. We see evidence of this is the papal Apostolic Exhortation on the crisis, which specifically attempts to narrate Western complicity in the climate crisis:

> "If we consider that emissions per individual in the United States are about two times greater than those of individuals living in China, and about seven times greater than the average of the poorest countries, we can state that a broad change in the irresponsible lifestyle connected with the Western model would have a significant long-term impact. As a result, along with indispensable political decisions, we would be making progress along the way to genuine care for one another."[11]

Perhaps few would dispute the common sense activism advocated by the Holy See. This advocacy highlights the manifold ways the climate crisis might be alleviated if Americans or Westerns would, at minimum, trade in SUVs for cars with lower emissions, for example. Furthermore, in a broader sense, this read properly recognizes western societies are disproportionate contributors to the material factors driving climate change. Such factors are incredibly disparate and irreducibly complex, evidenced by an examination

---

8   Bruce H. Wilkinson, "Humans as Geologic Agents: A Deep-Time Perspective," *Geology* 33, no. 3 (2005): 3.
9   Wilkinson, "Humans as Geologic Agents," 3.
10 Wilkinson, "Humans as Geologic Agents," 3.
11 Francis, *Holy Father. Apostolic Exhortation: Laudate Deum*, 15.

into the disproportionate amount of beef Americans consume, and its consequential effects, from factory to table, on climate change.[12]

But is lifestyle alteration and the alleviation it promises all that can be said? Though climate apocalypse activisms that highlight the possibility of extinction may be immediately effective towards capturing a sense of urgency and creating a consensus sufficient for political action, lies the question of whether both climate denialism, understood as resistance towards legislated extinction activisms, and climate activism across the post-Christian West reflect an inability to narrate the crisis itself in its entirety. Here at the borders and limits of such discourses, the church-community finds itself in a unique position, by virtue of its apocalyptic and messianic determination to give a responsible witness.

Climate Crisis as the Sin of Pride

The church-community tells the world what it does not know.[13] If the church is to be agent of reconciliation amidst the Anthropocene, this involves, paradoxically, a preemptive proclamation of good news in the midst of provisional facts. This pre-emptive proclamation is disciplined not by the encroaching possibility of extinction, but rather by the revelation of Christ in history. This proclamation of good news always illumines – anywhere and everywhere – the fragmentary facts of guilt, those shards of sin, death, and evil which the disclosure of Christ demarcates by its defeat in Hell.

Locating the climate crisis and the Anthropocene theologically begins by reading it in this apocalyptic dawn of Christ, not as a doomsday extinction narrative with attending activisms. The Anthropocene is but a novel manifestation of that ancient human situation of pride with its architectures of Babels it endlessly constructs, such efforts have been demarcated and defeated. The grounds for reading this novel material manifestation – that is the Anthropocene – as pride specifically in Barth's account of sin.

---

12 Amelia Willits-Smith et al., "Demographic and Socioeconomic Correlates of Disproportionate Beef Consumption among US Adults in an Age of Global Warming," *Nutrients* 15, no. 17 (August 30, 2023): 3795.

13 "The real church is by nature not an end in itself, but serves God by serving all men. Even when it withdraws to its interior lines, retreat can and will be merely the preparation for an all the more powerful appeal to the outside world [...] it is the duty of the really church to tell and show the world what it does not yet know" (Karl Barth, *Against the Stream: Shorter Post-War Writings, 1946–52* [London: SCM Press, 1954], 73).

Barth treats sin in three dimensions: pride, of sloth, and falsehood.[14] Pride is the primal origination for human sin, evidenced by mankind's usurpation of the knowledge of good and evil towards the realization of dominion in rebellion to the Creator. This narration however is solely and ultimately disclosed in the event of Easter. For this article, this means that the church-community's narration of guilt and sin (and the political actions it coordinates) is distinct from the moralization of material facts which factor into social, scholarly, or political consensus of climate crisis.

Material facts relative to accounts of climate crisis are not the basis for or the content of theological and ethical reflection. Rather, the disclosure of Christ furnishes the church with a theological logic and grammar, referring accounts of injustice or inequity of the Anthropocene, these fragments of guilt, to the landscape of Christian theology. Here, these fragments of injustice and inequity, ignorance and want, are not read merely in terms of classical vices like greed, but theologically as sin.

Reading material facts as guilt and sin is consequential to the church-community's own determination and confession, its primal witness to Jesus as Lord. In this framework wherein Barth's conception of guilt is a not merely a gulf of separation, but an existential, carceral state. A gripping summary is found in Church Dogmatics IV/1 §60:

> "We are in darkness before a wall which can be pierced only from the other side. There can be no question of any thought of redemption which we can manipulate, any capacity for redemption which we can put into effect. There is no stay or comfort in the idea of a freedom and capacity (which are finally and effectively ours) to look at ourselves as the man of sin from without, to take ourselves by the hand and to re-interpret and change ourselves. Knowledge of sin at this point consists in the knowledge: I am this man. But this knowledge of sin takes place in the knowledge of Christ."[15]

I want to suggest a faithful reading of Barth's account of sin recognizes that, for Barth, knowledge of guilt arises only from knowledge of Christ. On this basis, the guilt of the Anthropocene is far more than the sum of ma-

---

14 I am grateful for the 40th International Barth Conference held in Münster, Germany in 2023, where C. J. Smits' excellent paper on Barth's doctrine of sin, and the corresponding comments on my own paper, provoked this section and my attempt to locate climate crisis in Barth's hamartiology. C. J. Smits, "Barth's Doctrine of Sin" (The 40th International Barth Conference, Münster, Germany, 2023).

15 Barth, *CD IV/1*, 490.

terial facts. It is the novel manifestation of humanity's prideful condition and its consequential captivity of man to what Barth refers to as chthonic "lordless" powers.[16] The disproportionate contribution of Western industrialized societies cannot be amended or alleviated with extinction activisms or technocratic solutions. Discriminating the material facts of climate change from theological reads of climate change is not a rejection of their provisional reality, but more a refusal to adopt their interpreted meaning and implied activisms. In this discrimination, the church-community is refusing to adopt such facts as a sufficient basis or content of the church-community's apocalyptic existence and witness.[17] This is why a Barthian nexus, which we now turn to sketch, can furnish the church-community with resources to conceive of its existence and its witness, coordinating actions in the social and political, in the face of the Anthropocene.

A Barthian Constellation of Resources

A church-community determined by apocalyptic theology and aspiring to bear witness as agents of reconciliation amidst climate crisis may find content for its witness in a constellation of dogmatic touchpoints across the theological landscape of Barth's project.

Such a constellation may find its orientation by Barth's own dogmatic locus, election in Christ. He writes in II/2, "we can never be too comprehensive as we attempt to understand the election of Jesus as the beginning of all things."[18] Thus, in the midst of fragmentary guilt and provisional material facts, the church-community must narrate the climate crisis and coordinate political action through endless Christological discipline.

This beginning is the decisive, consummate apocalypse – disclosure – of God's judgement and grace towards man in the mystery of the God-man Christ-Jesus. This is the grounds from which Barth later states that even in the reality of "godless" men, the church and the world will never be addressed by a "manless" God.[19] We are not speaking then of the end of the world, but its beginning. This is the starting point for a church as agents of

---

16 Barth, *CD IV/4 Fragments*, 213–232.
17 I am indebted to one of my supervisors, Brian Brock, for this point on accounts of Christian ethics.
18 Barth, *CD II/2*, 126.
19 Barth, *Against the Stream*, 73.

reconciliation amidst the Anthropocene – the so-called "end of the world" as narrated by the popular lexicon.

On Election: Solidarity in Christ

Barth's doctrine of election, for the case we are considering here regarding the material situation of the Anthropocene, is the determination for Christian proclamation, not climate crisis. Election grounds the Church's proclamation to face this novel situation by reading it as a revolution of man's rebellion, novel but also demarcated in Christ. This narration and proclamation might be startling, but also bracing, like Barth's counsel during the rise of National Socialism, that the churches ought "to continue as if nothing had happened," the same can be true of the Church in the catastrophe and polycrisis of climate change.[20]

Second, the doctrine of election furnishes the Church with a thicker account of the guilt of the West. This transforms fragmentary facts into a theological narration, illuminated by a fundamental "Yes" proper to the church's proclamation. It is a "yes" that discloses nothing less than God with humanity, and humanity for one another. As Bonhoeffer notes "the world, even the lost world, is being ceaselessly drawn into the event of Christ."[21] This unity is free to implicate the disproportionate guilt of the West, narrating it as pride proper to its own construction of society and the colonial extension of its logics, economic, social and political, while retaining a solidarity with any and all "others."

Barth's account of election furnishes the church with responsibility in and for the world, not an escape hatch which pits church against world. It suggests a profound solidarity brought about by the grace and judgement of God in Christ. As the Church encounters material accounts of guilt as fragmentary facts – like that which the Holy See called the "irresponsible lifestyle of the Western model" – it can brace itself to proclaim solidarity which arises from election and salvation. This accommodates the perception of guilt in the social and political, while preserving the depths towards which the love of Christ has gone, the depths which is often obscured by political activism. Whatever guilt arises from the theological dimensions of climate crisis, the church is there to see and say God is *with* man contending with the climate

---

20 Barth, *Against the Stream*, 118.
21 *DBWE*, 17.

crisis, because Christ is with humankind in her election. But how does this election expand outward into creation according to Barth? How might this expansion serve our constellation of resources to assist the church-community in the Anthropocene?

On Creation: History and Extinction

A question here emerges in our navigation across Barth's dogmatic landscape. Can the climate crisis, with its material accounts of environmental decay and risk of mass extinction, have a place in Barth's doctrines of sin and creation? A glance at Barth's account in CD III/1 is helpful. His doctrine of creation begins by configuring the covenant of election as the internal basis of Creation, and Creation as the corresponding external basis of the covenant. Specifically, he writes,

> "[Creation] makes [covenant] technically possible; that it prepares and establishes the sphere in which the institution and history of the covenant take place; that it makes possible the subject which is to be God's partner in this history, in short the nature which the grace of God is to adopt and to which it is to turn in this history."[22]

One might claim this account of creation is too positivist, too abstract and strictly conceptual, with no way of speaking to materiality. This would signal a gap between creation, as understood by Barth, and climate crisis. If creation as such is a theological claim, perceived in faith (Hebrews 11:3), the question is whether such a hermeneutic can generate not just positively, but also concretely, any ethical content for the church's witness amidst material decay and extinction scenarios.

Creation in Barth's project gives the church-community hermeneutical grounds to narrate the material crisis of climate change without handing over and conforming its witness to activisms which pathologize theological narration. Creation, for Barth, is not the natural world, but rather theological theatre, the stage of salvation history apocalypsed in Jesus Christ. This recognition enables the church-community to both embrace responsibility in view of material devastation while giving witness to a God who sustains Creation by the Word of Christ. (Colossians 1:16-17)

---

22 Barth, *CD III/1*, 91.

Such a witness disrupts the anthropocentric activisms which assume independent and immediate responsibility to act – and ultimately – to save. Humanity, in its pride, is not the measure of all things. Rather, the reconciling Christ is for man, as Christ is for all the cosmos. This Christological point is crucial for a church-community that finds itself responsible in an age of climate change. Clough raises this point particularly from the dimension of creaturely existence:

> "despite the anthropocentric exuberance [...] arising from perceived common ground between Christianity and Greek philosophy in the Patristic period, or from new visions of human technological power in the early modern period, the better of the theological argument has always been on the side of those recognizing the importance of affirming the purpose of creation in a theocentric context."[23]

Barth's account of Creation will bear witness to the cosmic dimensions of God's covenant. The basis of Creation is that it a reality distinct *from* God, but that it is also *for* the God who is for man. God's electing solidarity with man does not make human beings the center of the cosmos, as extinction activisms or technocratic solutions presume.

The theological significance of this dimension of our constellation – a theocentric account of Creation – disrupts the moral activisms which often attends the Anthropocene which is as follows: if man is the villain, man must become the hero. This humanism is not the humanism which arises from the mystery of the gospel, the meaning or basis of creation.

And theological ethics, directing its efforts towards climate crisis is often trapped within and conditioned by these anthropocentrisms. Conradie recognizes this in his criticism of the stewardship language which often attends Christian activism towards climate crisis noting that

> "a theology of stewardship can all too easily be reduced to imply the maintenance of the present order, without recognising the Christian vision for the transformation of the whole of creation."[24]

Barth's doctrine of Creation, far from being an abstracted positivism, devoid of any concrete theological trajectory for the church faced with physical

---

23 David L. Clough, *On Animals: Systematic Theology: Volume I* (London / New York: Continuum, 2011), 19–20.
24 Ernst Conradie, *Christianity and Ecological Theology: Resources for Further Research*. Study Guides in Religion and Theology (Stellenbosch: African Sun Media, 2006), 133.

deterioration of the environment, delimits warped theological activisms that fail to account for the groaning of Creation under the Anthropocene for the renewal of all things.

These activisms either trade on the anthropocentrism reflected in the material reality of the Anthropocene or deploy "stewardship" language towards its preservation, denying the expansive and revolutionary elements released in the apocalypse of God's love for man in Christ. These activisms, as a consequence, are limited in their accounting for the guilt at the heart of Anthropocentric climate change. The material devastation of Creation is an element of pride against Creator. By obscuring the extent and direction of guilt, it is equally difficult to imagining a corresponding responsibility. This is the church-community's offer in such a constellation, to raise questions of responsibility and possibility that current activisms of "climate apocalypse" obscure by their own denial of the elements of the Christian apocalyptic witness. To imagine such responsibility, it is necessary to integrate the elective and Creative elements of our constellation with a formative element from Barth's doctrine of reconciliation.

On Reconciliation: Prayer and Revolt

The question is how and in what manner a church-community determined by elective solidarity amidst creation sustained by God's salvation and deliverance finds itself responsible in an age of climate crisis. Such a responsibility becomes clearer in a final integration of the first two doctrinal elements of our constructed Barthian constellation, election and creation, with Barth's account of reconciliation, particularly prayer and revolt. These elements, formative aspects proper to the Christian life, bring both vitality and concrete responsibility – ethical content – in view of the ethical questions pressing in on humankind in an age of climate change.

To summarize our constellation, first, in election, God reveals Himself in solidarity with humankind, He is "for her". This solidarity does not deny particular guilt by destroying the binary by which guilty parties justify themselves. Second, Creation is *for* God in serving as host to the history of salvation. In view of such solidarity and responsibility, questions of environmental decay and dangers of extinction, for example, of rising sea levels and its effect on indigenous or economically disadvantaged coastal communities, cannot be dismissed or denied by the church-community. Created by the Spirit of Jesus, it will find no ground to entertain evacuation from responsibility. Instead, by both its election and presence in creation, it will find itself free and responsible in its role as agents of reconciliation as witnesses to God's salvation.

The church-community realizes its role as agent of reconciliation through practices of prayer. In *The Christian Life*, Barth expounds on the Lord's Prayer as the defining horizon for the Christian life. He contends that prayer, as the practice of the Christian life, is

> "what God permits man, what he expects, wills, and requires of him, [...] a life of calling upon him. This life of calling upon God will be a person's Christian life: his life in freedom, conversion, faith, gratitude, and faithfulness."[25]

Jüngel summarizes this human side of Barth's conception of theological ethics as simply "instruction in prayer."[26] Prayer as a practice characterizes the worship of the church-community. It cultivates a posture of receptivity to the Word, making possible the "renewal of our minds" (Romans 12:1-2). Such a living, renewing community might resist by its very nature a reduction into-ideology by its Spiritual constitution as a defined space wherein the church encounters its Lord amidst the Anthropocene. The distinction between prayer in a Barthian frame and piety here becomes most essential, as the latter becomes a shelter for all sorts of denial or dismissal, while the former engenders the church-community to witness and participation in God's kingdom amidst the world. I want to suggest one outcome of this existence which is salient for an age of climate change, as Barth claims, necessitates a form of revolt which is salient for a church-community as agents of reconciliation.

Barth links prayer in the Christian life with a revolt rooted in praying "Thy Kingdom come." This "militant revolt demanded of Christians [...] is not directed against people: not even against the host of unbelievers" but rather against the "lordless" powers, that struggle against "the human plight" without which the church could not call itself the militant church.[27] The prayers of the church-community are the most primal expression of its eschatological hope. Such a hope, Barth reminds us, is nothing less than a revolt in and against this present age, while remaining resolutely for the world

---

25   Karl Barth, *The Christian Life*, Cornerstones Series (London / Oxford / New York / New Delhi / Sydney: Bloomsbury T&T Clark, 2017), 75-76
26   Eberhard Jüngel, *Theological Essays II*, trans. Arnold Neufeldt-Fast and John B. Webster (London: Bloomsbury, 2014), 164.
27   Barth, *CD IV/4*, 210–213.

as agents of reconciliation to the world. This revolt is according to its own reconciled form, the crucified yet risen body of Jesus Christ. Far from being an escape hatch from questions of climate change, of a gnostic referral to a transcendent God, the crucified body of Christ gives witness to God's subjection to the decay which pervades Creation. This Word is imperceptible outside of faith, and yet, in the revolt of the church-community that prays "Thy kingdom come", a reconciled witness is given to the body of Jesus which can generate responsibility and contribute to the shaping of a political consensus sufficient to act. This occurs as the church displays within itself the logic and concrete life of the reign of God, of the confession of sin, the provision of economic goods for those in need, and the recognition of fundamental political belonging and equality.[28]

Agents of Reconciliation Amidst the Anthropocene

This Barthian nexus of election, creation, and reconciliation disciplines the church-community towards acts of narration in view of the climate crisis which recovers two essential dimensions of Christian proclamation and witness: that God is *for* man, and that Creation is *for* God. Because of this, the *revolt* of the Church of which Barth speaks is itself an act reflective of reconciliation, revolting against not merely the destructive enslaving tendencies of man's irresponsible, prideful eradication of the material world, the meaning of which is perceived in faith as the theatre of divine glory. But it is also a revolt proper to man in his responsibility against sin, evil, and death – that which has been disclosed and disarmed, demarcated at Easter, yet still rages in its defeat. Such powers would seek only to have man believe that the Anthropocene's problem is also its solution. This can only recapitulate the chaos of Leviathan and mammon.

For the church to be an agent of reconciliation, it must remember God's gracious elective solidarity with humanity. It must recognize this dimension of election within Creation, as its decisive basis. In view of environmental decay, it cannot turn a blind eye to mass human migrations and the economic deprivations which will attend this crisis. Such a poly-crisis can only be addressed by the church-community insofar as its narration of the crisis and

---

28 On this point, see Hans G. Ulrich, particularly on adoption as God's children understood as a form of theological citizenship which disrupts normative accounts which trade on discourses of inclusion and exclusion. Ulrich, *Transfigured Not Conformed*, 253-278.

its corresponding ethical content arises from its own particular language and existence, one determined by the gospel. This Word confronts and disposes the church itself – its structures, practices, et cetera – from the ways in which it fuels climate crisis itself. Doing this the church becomes an agent of reconciliation in the midst of this crisis, tying itself to the good news of God's event in Jesus. The church-community is founded on the divestment of illusions, of a "renewing of our minds" according to what Paul calls the "logic" or "rationality" of our worship. (Romans 12:1-2) This renewal is always rooted in a decisive apocalypse of Jesus as Lord, even and especially in an age appropriately called the Anthropocene.

Barth Graduate Student Colloquium

2023

Morgan Bell

Rightly or Wrongly, Speaking the Father
Barth, Gender Performativity, and Patriological Analogy

"Gender is a complexity whose totality is permanently deferred, never fully what it is at any given juncture in time."[1]

I. Toward a Cataphatic, Discursive Patriology

There are dangers inherent to naming and invoking the First Person of the Trinity. In her *God, Sexuality, and the Self*, Sarah Coakley communicates these dangers well and sums up the spirit of much theology on this topic: "'the medium is the message' in the way we subliminally message God," she writes, and by those media and messages we "can mandate and remandate repressive patriarchy even as some other (supposedly enlightened) message is being announced rhetorically from the pulpit or podium."[2] When Christians pray to or invoke God the Father, much less enter the sphere of patriology,[3] they enter into the thick of cisheteropatriarchal regimes. Decades of feminist and womanist (and increasingly queer) scholarship has demonstrated that what may appear to be purely dogmatic assertions or doxological statements are produced by and themselves produce social, political, sexed, and gendered realities and consequences.

---

1   Judith Butler, *Gender Trouble: Feminism and the Subversion of Identity* (New York: Routledge, 1990), 22.
2   Sarah Coakley, *God, Sexuality, and the Self* (Cambridge: Cambridge University Press, 2013), 322.
3   Whereas Robert Jenson opts for "patrology" and Ryan Ripee for "paterology," I use "patriology" to denote the doctrine of God the Father. Among its other potential strengths, this term serves to distinguish the doctrine from the study of patristic theology. See Robert Jenson, *Systematic Theology*, vol. 1 (New York: Oxford University Press, 1997), 115; Ryan L. Rippee, *That God May Be All in All* (Eugene, OR: Pickwick Publications, 2018).

Yet by Coakley's lights, to simply revise or replace traditional naming conventions for God the Father (independent of the theological and Scriptural questions this move raises) simply does not go far enough in redressing these deleterious consequences. "The demons" of gendered God-talk, she contends, "have to be slain one by one, and indeed over and over; and it is the task of us all to slay our own demons."[4] Per Sigmund Freud, to kill the father is simply to reinstate his rule. The popular response of trading "masculine" terms (e.g., "Father") for "feminine" (e.g., "Mother") or supposedly ungendered ones (e.g., "Creator") perhaps simply masks rather than roots out the hegemonic and sexed/gendered dimensions of God-talk. In response, Coakley counsels a Spirit-led, prayer-born askesis that leads to "a 'Fatherhood' beyond patriarchalism."[5] Thereby, the one who prays is brought to bask in an seemingly unthematizable "ray of divine darkness" (in the vein of Pseudo-Denys) that is the Father's true nature.[6] Praying with the Son in the Spirit, thereby participating in the taxis of desire and self-offering that just *is* triune life, "our presumptions about 'Fatherhood' strangely start to change […] and at last we follow Jesus into an exploration of the meaning of 'Fatherhood' beyond all human formulations."[7] Aberrative and humanly-determined notions of divine Paternity are refashioned "in the purgative kneeling before the blankness of the darkness which nonetheless dazzles": sanctifying the knowledge of the one who prays through "noetic slippage."[8] And in this process, Coakley trusts, patriarchal patriologies are slain ever anew.

While I am more sympathetic to Coakley than she,[9] Linn Marie Tonstad asks a crucial question of Coakley's ascetical and (I contend) ultimately non-

---

4   Coakley, *God, Sexuality, and the Self*, 323.
5   Ibid., 332.
6   Ibid., 323.
7   Ibid., 326.
8   Ibid., 325.
9   In many important respects, I am sympathetic to Tonstad's vociferous critique of Coakley in her *God and Difference: The Trinity, Sexuality, and the Transformation of Finitude* (New York: Routledge, 2016). I too find "corrective projectionism" of limited social and political use, reifying as it often does hegemonic human relations, and that it conflates anthropology, human relationality, and the divine life. I agree that Coakley is not always as careful as she might be to distinguish destructive and purgative sufferings (though not all suffering, I would argue, is not of a piece). I too worry that Coakley elides Christ and the redeemed creature in Christ (reminiscent of a Troeltschian *gestalt* christology). Theologians do well to attend to Tonstad's critiques. Nonetheless, I am less sure of Tonstad's proposed alternatives. To reconfigure trinitarian taxes along the lines of "gift circulation" instead of relations of origin seems to recast rather than undo the very relations Tonstad

discursive apprehension of the First Person: "must not these noetic consequences be recognized by the pray-er? Otherwise, how would Coakley know that her idolatries were being eradicated?"[10] For in Coakley's telling, genuine patriological knowledge is largely unthematizable, given the free subjectivity of its object as encountered in spiritual practice as well as the embodied reformation of human knowledge. Yet by what standards, by which patriological criteria, does Coakley adjudicate between faithful and idolatrous patriologies? How would an ascetic and apophatic patriology avoid lapsing into equivocation? Tonstad rightly notes that the theologian is "compelled to recognize idolatrous slippage between one form of fatherhood and another."[11] To do so, however, at least on some level implies discursive, cataphatic knowledge of God the Father; the ability to name the analogies and disanalogies between creaturely and divine paternities. To flesh out that knowledge, however, runs the risk of instating and reinstating the very aberrative and hegemonic patriologies Coakley is right to decry. This is perhaps why many shrink from or work around explicitly naming what is particularly "fatherly" about the Father of our Lord Jesus Christ. To give discursive content to the hallowed Name is to run the great risk of sedimenting and absolutizing hegemonic cisheteropatriarchy.

Recognizing the seriousness of the enterprise, this article will argue that this is a risk dogmatics must take – and take up continually. In addition to the tasks of patriological knowledge, witness, and confession to which Christ calls his disciples (John 17), to "slay the demons" of cisheteropatriarchy "over and over" requires those demons to be unmasked, named, and thus exposed to exorcism by the power of the One whose authority they seek to usurp. Patrology (quite beyond naming conventions for the First Person) *always* risks installing and concretizing hegemonic masculinities; that is a cardinal

---

seeks to critique (228ff). Moreover, her recommendation of Friedrich Schleiermacher's trinitarianism (particularly his anti-speculative and exceedingly spare conception of the immanent Trinity) presents at least three dogmatic risks Tonstad wishes to avoid: (1) undermining Christian assurance that the God who graces "slaves with sonship" is a reliable and self-consistent God; (2) depending how far Tonstad wishes to go with Schleiermacher (she leaves this open-ended), she runs the risk of slipping back into hierarchical trinitarian relationship given Schleiermacher's near-equation of the Son with "passivity" and the Father with "activity"; and (3) she risks masking, rather than exposing, potentially problematic features of trinitarianism that she sees as baked into the subterranean architecture of trinitarian dogma.

10 Coakley, *God, Sexuality, and the Self,* 102.
11 Ibid., 5.

reason why dogmatics *must* articulate and rearticulate it. Cisheteropatriarchal demons can be slain only by proffering patriological proposals and by the Church's critical assessment and appropriation of them. To do so, an account must be given of the terms of the analogical relationship between God the Father and human fathers – the terms of engagement between divine and creaturely fathers must be established. This essay will argue for an apocalyptic, performative *analogia fidei* between divine and creaturely fathers that at once possibilizes discursive speech about the First Person of the Trinity and that also contains dogmatic resources to critique the hegemonic patriarchy that has long beset patriology.

First, this essay will begin by engaging Karl Barth's account of the analogical relationship between creaturely and divine paternities. Barth offers conceptual resources for pursuing a discursive patriology of which gender ideological critique could be a constitutive feature. Then, this essay will examine some ways in which Barth's reading of the Father/fathers relation still retains elements of an *analogia entis* rather than an *analogia fidei* and the patriological and gender-political risks this vestige poses. It will then revise his account in light of Judith Butler's performative understanding of gender and sexuality, arguing for a discursive patriology which at once respects the Father's self-revelation in the Son while supporting Coakley's stated goal of slaying the demons that pretend to divine Paternity. The confines of this essay prohibit a full account of what it means to call upon the First Person as "Father." Rather, the goal will be to clarify the analogical relationship between divine and creaturely fathers so that such work might be pursued.

II. The Father and fathers: Critiquing Barth with Barth

At every step in his *Church Dogmatics*, Barth is at assiduous pains to continually delineate Creator from creature. The effective protection against eliding the creature with its Creator is the sovereign self-revelation of God in Jesus Christ as attested in the Scriptures. In Christ Jesus, God encounters the creature as its Lord. This event of revelation is where God decisively reveals Godself. The incarnate Word of the Father, then, proves the only reliable Cornerstone upon which Christian theology can be built. Thus, Barth categorically rules out any "natural patriology" as though the first article could be a "forecourt of the Gentiles." There can be no patriology *remoto Christo* as though the First Person were an abstract, generic deity rather than the Father of the eternal Son who became human for the sake of humanity. Theologians, therefore, cannot proceed as though the Father were "directly accessible to us and that only the truth of the second article needs a revelation."[12] A patrology so construed would proceed without reference to the Son. The Father's identity would be commonplace knowledge inherent in human experience or creaturely reality, even if it were sharpened by Christ's teaching, and thus liable to projectionism or idolatry.

Pace such approaches, Barth makes the strong claim that Jesus "revealed the *unknown* Father, *His* Father, and in so doing, and only in so doing, He told us *for the first time* that the Creator is, what He is, and that He is as such our Father."[13] Nothing – not creaturely fatherhood, not the character of creation, not providence – should be considered *sub specie aeternitatis* save by reference to the Eternal One who became timeful for us. Creaturely fatherhood, for example, does not bespeak divine Paternity *ex opere operato*. The Father of lights is obscured from the creature save by the light that radiates from the One at the right hand of Power.

To see the Father, therefore, one must see the Son to whom the Father is inextricably bound from all eternity in the communion of their Spirit. Put unartfully: in both the economy and God's immanent life, the Father is analytic in the Son. Patriological knowledge is secured only by serious and spiritual appropriation of the biblical witness "to the degree that formally it absolutely conditions and binds the content of the revelation of the Father by its impartation in the person of the Revealer Jesus of Nazareth. Its content cannot be abstracted from this form."[14] Christ, as scripturally attested, does not merely teach *about* the Father. He is not one instantiation (potentially among

---

12 Karl Barth, *Dogmatics in Outline*, trans. G.T. Thomson (New York: Harper & Row, 1959), 50.
13 Barth, *CD* I/1, 391. Emphasis added. Barth's comments about the novelty of Jesus' revelation of the Father stand in an interpretive line extending back to at least the late nineteenth century, and presage Joachim Jeremias' exegetical work arguing the same (See the latter's *Abba: Studien zur neutestamentlichen Theologie und Zeitgeschichte* and *Neutestamentliche Theologie*). Jeremias' contention that Jesus' use of "Abba" was "childish" and bespoke the intimacy Jesus enjoyed with God has come under serious scrutiny (see James Barr, "Abba Isn't 'Daddy,'" *The Journal of Theological Studies* 39, no. 1 [April 1988]: 28–47). Moreover, other scholars have refuted Jeremias' claim that Jesus' *invocation* of God as Father represents a novel development vis-à-vis Second Temple Judaism; demonstrating the term's limited but well-established usage (see Marianne Meye Thompson, *The Promise of the Father: Jesus and God in the New Testament* (Louisville, KY: Westminster John Knox Press, 2000), 21–55).
14 Barth, *CD* I/1, 390.

many) of a generic sonship. As the repetition in time of the *repitio aeternitatis in aeternitate*, the content of revelation (say, Christ's teaching about the Father or patriological "principles" distilled from the Gospel narratives) cannot be divorced from revelation's form with the content "regarded as divine and necessary and the form as human and contingent."[15] Jesus of Nazareth is identical with the only and eternally Begotten. Thus, for the First Person to be Father is precisely to be Father of *this One*. The Son's life is, in a qualified sense, the discursive content of the Father's such that "God is unknown as our Father, as the Creator, to the degree that He is not made known by Jesus."[16] As such, "we have to learn [God's] fatherhood from the will of God fulfilled on and by Jesus."[17] To see the Son is to see the Father (John 14:9).

For Barth, then, there can be no question of amplifying creaturely conceptions of fatherhood and applying them to the first Mode of divine being. God's Fatherhood must remain "unconfused by recollection of other fatherhoods" (… *ohne Verwirrung durch die Erinnerung an andere Väterlichkeiten*…).[18] Instead, asserts Barth, the theologian must respect that divine paternity *somehow* grounds and conditions creaturely paternity. Marshalling Ephesians 3:15 in an interpretive tradition that stretches back to at least Athanasius,[19] Barth contends that

> "it is from God's fatherhood that our natural human fatherhood acquires any meaning and dignity it has (*Sondern von der Vaterschaft Gottes her bekommt die menschlich-natürliche Vaterschaft das, was ihr an Sinn und Würde zukommt*). God is the Father ἐξ οὗ πᾶσα πατριὰ ἐν οὐρανοῖς καὶ ἐπὶ γῆς ὀνομάζεται ['from whom all fatherhood in heaven and on earth takes its name']."[20]

Now, one might make much of Barth's contention that human paternity *acquires* "meaning and dignity" from divine paternity. As the Word "which aims at us and smites us in our existence,"[21] one might expect Barth to say that the revelatory Word of the Father graciously elects creaturely father-

---

15 Barth, *CD I/1*, 390.
16 Barth, *CD I/1*, 390.
17 Barth, *CD I/1*, 391f.
18 Barth, *KD I/1*, 413.
19 For Athanasius, created reality bears the imprint of divine reality given their causal relationship. Thus, the fullest and deepest expression of reality generally and fatherhood particularly is found in God. See Peter Widdicombe, *The Fatherhood of God from Origen to Athanasius* (Oxford: Clarendon Press, 1994), 177.
20 Barth, *CD I/1*, 389.
21 Barth, *CD I/1*, 149.

hood, reconstituting and extending it beyond its natural capacities for the purpose of speaking of (indeed, *to*) a divine Referent to whom it could never of its own resources refer.[22] "Acquisition," then, would denote the Father's imputation of divine communicability to creaturely conceptions and instantiations of fatherhood: a "commandeering," fatherhood's being slain and made alive for a specific revelatory vocation. But Barth himself casts doubt on this interpretation. The Father, he writes in 1935 (three years after the publication of the materials from *KD* I/1 analyzed above), "reveals Himself to us and is the incomparable *prototype* of all human creaturely fatherhood: 'from whom every fatherhood (πᾶσα πατριὰ) in heaven and earth is named' (Eph. 3:15)."[23] Yet what are the terms of the Father's analogical relation to creaturely fathers? With reference to the same passage from Ephesians, Thomas Aquinas argued that a *natural* relation exists between the Father and fathers – the latter are analogical, ontological copies of the former.[24] Thus for Thomas, while respecting the differences between Creator and creature, God's Fatherhood ontologically precedes and grounds human fatherhood, but noetically the Father is the *perfection* of the paternal existence they instantiate. Thus, the Father is both *arche* and *telos* of human paternity.

---

22 For the mature Barth, patriological speech is primarily invocative: a graced calling upon the Father of Jesus Christ. The Son alone calls upon the Father as "Father" by rights. To the extent that Christians pray to "*our* Father," this is a gift of adoptive grace made effective for them by the unitive work of the Holy Spirit. For an exploration of this in the context of Barth's doctrine of prayer – and account attentive to the political corollaries of Barth's theology – see Ashley Cocksworth, *Karl Barth on Prayer* (London: T&T Clark, 2015), 83–120.

23 Karl Barth, *Credo* (New York: Chas. Scribner's Sons, 1962), 24. Emphasis added. In the lectures that comprised *Dogmatics in Outline*, Barth holds that "true and proper fatherhood resides in God, and from this Fatherhood of God what we know as fatherhood among us men is derived. The divine Fatherhood is the primal source of all natural fatherhood. As is said in Ephesians, every fatherhood in heaven and on earth is of Him" (Barth, *Dogmatics in Outline*, 43).

24 Thomas Aquinas, *Summa Theologiae*, Ia q33. George Hunsinger helpfully defines "*analogia entis*," at least in Barth's understanding: it "is conceived as embracing two matters at once: a constitutive state of affairs and an epistemic procedure based on it [...]. The state of affairs is one in which human beings are in some sense inherently open to and capable of knowing God. The procedure is then one in which this inherent openness and capacity are exercised such that God becomes known, regardless of how provisionally" (Hunsinger, *How to Read Karl Barth: The Shape of His Theology* [New York: Oxford University Press, 1991], 283f).

With Thomas, Barth maintains that the Father's paternity is grounded solely in the fact

> "that in Jesus and Jesus alone He is manifest as the Creator and therefore as our Father [and] it follows that He already is that which corresponds thereto antecedently and in Himself, namely, in His relation to the One through whom He is manifested, and therefore in His relation to Jesus."[25]

The Father's relation qua Creator is dependent on the Father's antecedent Paternity of the Son in such a way that suggests a distinction between the two. Thus Barth acknowledges that, as a creaturely artifact, the identificatory signifier "father" has a special character when used in reference to the First Person: "Faith in God the Father must be proclaimed in such a way that implicitly, at once, and unconfused by recollection of other fatherhoods, faith in the only-begotten Son must be impressed upon the hearers."[26] Given the infinite qualitative difference between God and the creation – a guiding motif present from the *Römerbrief* through Barth's mature works – he does not wish to establish such a seamless relationship between heavenly and earthly paternities.

But lest the name "Father" fall into equivocation for fear of ontological analogy, Barth elaborates that "the Creator is the standard of what is proper for the creature and therefore for our language too."[27] He writes that

> "if we call God Father, it is because he is Father in reality. And the relation between God's Fatherhood and fatherhood among men reverses itself: we do not call God Father because we know what this is; on the contrary, *because we know God's Fatherhood we afterwards understand what human fatherhood is*. The divine truth precedes and grounds the human truth."[28]

It is not – as with Friedrich Schleiermacher – that "father" names the quality of a relation experienced by the human subject vis-à-vis God. Humans do not reflect upon their own fatherly experiences and apply them to God. Rather, God is antecedently Father in a way that sheds new and revelatory light on the inner constitution of creaturely paternity.

---

25 Barth, *CD I/1*, 391.
26 Barth, *CD I/1*, 392.
27 Barth, *CD I/1*, 392.
28 Barth, *The Faith of the Church,* trans. Gabriel Vahanian (New York: Meridian Books, 1958), 14. Emphasis added.

Yet does this reversal go sufficiently far given Barth's concerns to demarcate divine and creaturely existences? For a somewhat loose example, consider Barth's treatment of Scripture and proclamation as creaturely forms of the Word of God. As creaturely media, Barth argues that the Bible and preaching are "not intrinsically but in virtue of the divine decision taken ever and anon [to continually become God's Word] as the free God uses them."[29] Their justified and sanctified vocation is restricted to their graced use by God in the event of revelation. By contrast, in that revelatory event and the human response to it, Barth suggests that divine Fatherhood somehow grants to or discloses already within human fatherhood a stable, abiding dignity that corresponds to the Father's own – implying a sort of *vestigium paternitatis*. In some sense, therefore, the First Person's Paternity can serve as the critical canon for assessing human fatherhood (which seems to be a citational copy of the former), yet Barth does not provide detail on what this looks like with any concretion.[30] Does God in Christ reveal, say, a *genetic* or *behavioural model* of paternity that fathers are to emulate? Or, as Barth seems to suggest here and elsewhere, does his revelation of the Father expose a *pre-existent correspondence* between the Father and fathers that was obscured but not wholly destroyed by sin?[31] By his own lights, revelation and the election of creaturely media to witness to the *res* of divine Being-in-Act should not simply *rehabilitate* but rather graciously *reconstitute* the creatures whom God encounters.

This, however, is precisely what Barth does not say of the paternal analogy. To remain consistent, then, Barth should insist rather that human fatherhood cannot be simply shown a better model of itself or healed by grace as though only partially deformed. It must be crucified and resurrected and still further graced if it can serve as the Father's self-reference ever anew. In the event of revelation, "fatherhood" must be graciously extended beyond its natural capacities so to refer to an Unknown God made known in Jesus

---

29 Barth, *CD* I/1, 117.
30 Such a conception is even more troubling given the connection Barth draws between intratrinitarian relations and sexed human relations. On this point, see Faye Bodley Dangelo, *Sexual Difference, Gender, and Agency in Karl Barth's* Church Dogmatics (London: T&T Clark, 2020), esp. 105–38.
31 Barth identifies the imago Dei with a "point of contact" by which "the humanity and personality of sinful man" could "signify conformity to God." The imago is not, for Barth, "destroyed apart from a few relics; it is totally destroyed" (*vernichtet*) (Barth, *CD* I/1, 239; *KD* I/1, 251).

Christ. Indeed, as Faye Bodley-Dangelo notes, "only through a divine act can the human subject become a copy of the divine 'prototype.'"[32] Only by the miracle of grace can creaturely conceptions of "fatherhood" refer to and name the eternal Father of the Son.

Given the unique use to which fatherhood is put in divine reference, it is unclear why Barth concludes that divine Paternity serves as a critical canon for *creaturely* paternities. Consider: As the Bible is graced to be Holy Scripture for human creatures, the Bible is not a critical canon for the true nature of books (except in perhaps the most abstract of ways); nor is the unique Sonship of Christ a model for human sonship apart from that into which human creatures are adopted by grace, and only then quite disanalogously. So why does human fatherhood receive such status? Absent an account on how divine fatherhood crosses the ontological divide between Creator and creature to graciously relate human fatherhood to his own, Barth risks implicitly repeating Thomas' ontological analogy between fathers and the Father. Barth gives no concrete account for how "fatherhood" is graciously remade in encounter with Jesus Christ so to correspond to the Father in faithful response and witness. This is what the *analogia fidei* would require.[33]

III. Patriology and Performative Paternity: A Destabilizing *Analogia Fidei*

The call for these dogmatic adjustments to the underpinnings of Barth's patriology take on increased import considering the repressive and destructive consequences of cisheterpatriarchal regimes alluded to above. In pursuing this line of analysis, I assume rather than argue for the performative view of gender articulated by Judith Butler.[34] In Butler's view, gender, sex, and identity (such as gendered family roles) are not "nouns." Rather, they are "verbs" such that "gender proves to be performative – that is, constituting the iden-

---

32 Bodley-Dangelo, *Sexual Difference, Gender, and Agency*, 127.
33 Hunsinger: "The *analogia fidei* [...] posits an analogy between a human action (faith) and a divine action (grace) in just a situation where no ontological commonality is conceived to exist. Grace elicits faith, and faith corresponds analogically to grace, but no ontological commonality of any kind mediates them" (Hunsinger, *How to Read Karl Barth*, 283f).
34 Judith Butler's *Gender Trouble: Feminism and the Subversion of Identity* (New York: Routledge, 1990) ignited a flurry of interest in gender performativity. See especially Idem., *Bodies That Matter: On the Discursive Limits of Sex* (New York: Routledge, 1993); Ellen Armour and Susan St. Ville, eds., *Bodily Citations: Religion and Judith Butler* (New York: Columbia University Press, 2006).

tity it is purported to be. In this sense, gender is always a doing, though not a doing by a subject who might be said to preexist the deed."[35] In this understanding, creaturely fatherhood (as a gender-indexed – better, gender-productive – and discursive phenomenon) is not embryonic as though fathers proleptically possess natural "fatherly features" which are then cultivated or quashed by external forces or the paternal subject's will. Rather, paternity and fathers are constituted precisely in repeating a series of stylized acts which a dominant social order has coded as indicative of paternity. Fathers are made, to echo Simone de Beauvoir, not born. This does not mean that fatherhood is "fake" or "artificial." "Performative" does not mean "illusory" or "fictive." Rather, creaturely fatherhood is the discursive product of "certain configurations of gender [that] take the place of 'the real' and consolidate and augment their hegemony through that felicitous self-naturalization."[36]

While this account of human paternity is developed with reference to Butler's account of performativity, it has generative resonances with Barth's dogmatic theology.[37] Even for Barth, creaturely fatherhood cannot be an innate or essential identity since, per his christological anthropology, all human existence – including sexed and gendered existence – is a "being in act": "a persistent activity to be conducted in obedience to the divine command and in constant negotiation of culturally contingent conventions."[38] Accordingly, paternity simply does not denote the exact same phenomenon observable in Second Temple Judaism nor mid-century American suburbia nor in life on an Annishabeg reserve in southern Ontario nor the realities of adoptive or gay or trans fatherhoods.[39] A variety of contingent pressures codify and recodify paternity such that "fatherhood" names not a "noun," but an ever-developing social reality. This is not to say that there is no such thing as hegemonic patriarchalism or that there is no culturally current "meaning" to paternity – these are indeed the products of paternal performances. Rather, it is to say that identarian categories are constantly reworked and reinscribed,

---

35 Butler, *Gender Trouble*, 34.
36 Butler, *Gender Trouble*, 45.
37 Here, as in other parts of this article, I rely on the incisive work of Faye Bodley-Dangelo.
38 Bodley-Dangelo, *Sexual Difference, Gender, and Agency*, 24.
39 As but one example, consider how adoptive paternity figures into the Scriptural depiction of God as Father and our redemption as children of God by grace. In revelation, I contend, God summons out discrete features of contingent human paternities and makes them to refer to divine realities to which they, by their own resources, cannot point. See Erin M. Heim, *Adoption in Galatians and Romans: Contemporary Metaphor Theories and the Pauline* Huiothesia *Metaphors* (Leiden: Brill, 2017).

policed and perturbed in a way that is never finalizable. Human paternities are "tenuously constituted in time, instituted in an exterior space through *a stylized repetition of acts*."[40] Human fatherhood is in constant flux.

Much more can be said of the political potential of subverting gender consolidations.[41] However, closer to our interests here is the reality that those consolidations *are* subverted, *are* subject to flux and contestation and restylization. Because this is so, human and divine paternities cannot be said to exist in a stable, consistent analogy of being: the Father whose being just is his pure and singular act of generation and spiration graciously relates himself to human paternities that themselves are neither stable nor consistent. That latter "fatherhood" (if it can be referred to in the singular) is not what it is at any given juncture in time. To posit or imply an *analogia entis* between the Father and creaturely fathers would be to ontologize and thus insidiously congeal but one calcified product of paternal construction and reconstruction. If there can be an analogy between the Father of the eternal Son and contingent, creaturely performances of paternity, it must be an *analogia fidei*; a graced relation in which the various constructions of creaturely paternity are "not intrinsically but in virtue of the divine decision taken ever and anon" to be made to communicate the Father's own self-naming "as the free God uses them."[42] The Father commandeers the features, meanings, attributes, expressions, and valences associated with the various contingent performances of paternity in such a way that

> "the relation of correspondence which is established in the revelation-event does not become a predicate of the human subject [...]. The analogy endures only so long as the revelation-event endures [...]. It must continue to be effected moment by moment by the sovereign action of the divine freedom if it is to be effected at all."[43]

Divine paternity, then, does "not become a predicate" of creaturely paternities. Such correspondences are established by God for the express and limited purposes of God's self-revelation. There is, therefore, no enduring essential or ontological bond between creaturely fathers and the Father in

---

40 Butler, *Gender Trouble*, 191.
41 Butler develops this application at length. See Idem., *Undoing Gender* (New York: Routledge, 2004).
42 Barth, *CD I/1*, 117.
43 Bruce McCormack, *Karl Barth's Critically Realistic Dialectical Theology: Its Genesis and Development 1909–1936* (Oxford: Oxford University Press, 1995), 17.

heaven; such bonds are forged in the apocalyptic fire of revelation, and are forged exclusively for use.

IV. Risking Patriology

If these are indeed the analogical terms at play in the Father-father relation, patriology becomes less a dogmatic locus that can be articulated once-for-all and more an ongoing hermeneutical project for the Church. In each age, each context, each congregation, each pray-er, we must discern which conceptions of paternity are being crucified and resurrected to refer to the Father and how, precisely, they are slain and graciously made alive. The patriological *analogia fidei*, then, is a never-concluded *event*. With Coakley, we can thus say that patriology is indeed a theology *in via* – but an apocalyptic *via*.

But this *via* cannot finally be a non-discursive or apophatic enterprise; to do so does not reckon with the Father's gracious address to us in Jesus Christ, the Father's self-display in the Father's will enacted on and in the Nazarene, nor does it adequately expose and rebel against the sinister uses to which cisheteropatriarchy constantly puts patriology. The Church must continually plumb the terms of the patriological analogy according to what we learn of God the Father as the Father's will and ways are made known in Jesus Christ, and in so doing name and excise all "natural patriologies" that rely upon naturalizing paternities. The Church must continually place its patriological discourse under the judgment of the Father's Word and, so doing, thereby offer something of a "political genealogy" of paternal ontologies. Such faithful hermeneutical analysis would contribute to the deconstruction of the "substantive appearance" of paternity "into its constitutive acts and locate and account for those acts within the compulsory frames set by the various forces that police the social appearance of gender."[44] And these demons must, as Coakley is right to note, be slain over and over.

This essay has offered a modest proposal as to how one might move toward a discursive patriology and critically engaged some of the terms that would guide such engagement with the doctrine of the First Person. What is missing, however, is the necessary second step of articulating the content of such a patriology: the sense in which the First Person is "fatherly," how the Father "commandeers" and graciously remakes current and widespread conceptions of paternity to witness to the Father's own being and work. This

---

44 Butler, *Gender Trouble*, 45.

is dogmatic work that, in contemporary trinitarian discourse, has only been taken up sporadically. Still, beyond these crucial concerns, theologians must pursue not just a theology of *naming* the First Person or analyses of the symbolic character of "Father language," but also a full-throated patriology: an account of the person and work of the first Mode of divine being. It is here that a substantive vision of Father (which we pray able to judge aberrative notions of divine Paternity) must be constructed. Admittedly, this is risky business. Theologians will consistently speak the Father *wrongly*. They will predicate not only idolatrous but dangerous things of the Father. But only in prosecuting the patriological task, and advisedly and strategically taking such risks, can the idols and dangers of patriology be brought into the Father's light of judgment and grace.

Frank Della Torre II

Church and State in Barth's Political Theology

Introduction

The relationship between church and state, the Christian community and the civil community, and the *civitas Dei* and the *civitas terrena* has been the subject of intense dispute within Christian theology from the very beginning. "Give to Caesar the things that are Caesar's and to God the things that are God's" (Mark 12:17). What this means is not easy to articulate. For what things belong to Caesar that human beings should give them to him? And what does Caesar possess that was not first given to him by God? Do not all things belong to God – including the things that apparently belong to Caesar? Is not Caesar *God's* possession? Where, then, do God's possessions stop and Caesar's start?

Such questions are not mere theological niceties. They impinge upon the central concerns of Christian faith and practice in the world, i.e., how to relate church and state in the life of the Christian. I propose in this article to examine how Karl Barth envisions the relation between church and state across a number of his essays. My goal is to examine the different ways Barth defines and relates these two institutions to better understand his political theology. Much scholarly attention has been devoted to explaining the development of Barth's dogmatic theology – its various (dis)continuities.[1] This paper aims to shed light upon whether one can detect continuity, discontinuity, or both in Barth's political theological conceptions of church/state relations.

Toward this end, three essays across Barth's corpus – spanning 35 years – will be examined that exemplify how he coordinates the relation between church and state. I should note at the fore that I am not interested in Barth's political views as they are shaped by whatever political or historical moment;

---

1 Cf. Chapter 1 in Eberhard Jüngel, *Karl Barth: A Theological Legacy*, trans. Garrett E. Paul (Philadelphia, PA: The Westminster Press, 1986).

rather, this essay seeks to shed light on the models or theories of church and state that Barth employs in his political theology. While Barth does not always use the language of "church" and "state" in these writings, he has these institutions or theological loci in view even when employing other names (e.g., the Christian, society, the civil community, social democracy, and so on). In addition to gaining more clarity about the nature and development of Barth's political theology, this essay will conclude by noting how Barth might be of continued use to us today as the relation between church and state is again being renegotiated in present society.

"Jesus Christ and the Movement for Social Justice" (1911)

The first lecture to be examined is Barth's early piece, "Jesus Christ and the Movement for Social Justice," first published in December, 1911 in the socialist daily of his canton, *Der Freie Aargauer*. In it, one encounters a younger Barth who is in some ways quite familiar, yet in others rather strange. His characteristic verve and penchant for playful but rigorous critique are certainly apparent. And yet, the reader may be somewhat surprised not to hear the strong tenor of all-encompassing judgment that will, a decade later, gain Barth his infamous notoriety upon the publication of *Der Römerbrief* (second edition).[2]

This early lecture employs a model of church/state relations that is rather distinct, if not wholly different, from later formulations. As will be discussed later in this essay, the church (defined as an institution), for the early Barth, is merely an instrument that can help – but oftentimes hinders – one's capacity to follow Jesus in the present. What is essential is not the church, but following the spirit of Jesus, which in the present looks like radically committing oneself to the movement for social justice as embodied in social democracy. At this early stage, the locus of Barth's political theology, in other words, is not in the church or in Christian dogma, but in the pursuit of social democratic ends in the realm of politics.

Barth opens his lecture with the claim that Jesus and the movement for social justice are one and the same: "Jesus *is* the movement for social justice, and the movement for social justice *is* Jesus in the present."[3] The two must

---

2   Karl Barth, *Der Römerbrief (Zweite Fassung) 1922* (Zürich: Theologischer Verlag Zürich, 1989).
3   Karl Barth, "Jesus Christ and the Movement for Social Justice," in *Karl Barth: Theologian of Freedom*, ed. Clifford Green (Minneapolis, MN: Fortress Press, 1991), 99.

be understood together, for the one implies the other. The "real contents" of the person of Jesus can be summarized by the words, "movement for social justice." Conversely, the social justice movement of the nineteenth and twentieth centuries are not only, Barth claims, "the greatest and most urgent word of God to the present," but are also "a quite direct continuation of the spiritual power which [...] entered into history and life with Jesus." Before defending this initial claim, Barth immediately addresses objections from two sides: the Christian-bourgeois camp and the socialist camp. Barth first anticipates that his Christian-bourgeois readers will object to associating Jesus with a particular political party. Jesus is not a Social Democrat, they will say. He is non-partisan, above and indifferent to social conflicts; his significance is eternal, not historically limited, which are the concerns of the social democratic party. This camp will claim that socialists have done terrible and shameful things in the name of their socialism.

Barth responds to these objections rather forcefully. What ultimately matters, he says, is not what socialists *do*, but what they *want*. One cannot discredit what socialists want by pointing out that they frequently fail to attain their ultimate goal or that the methods employed by this or that socialist are out of step with their political and economic aims. In fact, what socialists want is in a sense timeless and quite beyond the various controversies of this or that political party or individual socialist. Quite simply put, what socialists want is the movement for social justice. With this clarification in view, Barth's goal in this lecture is "to demonstrate the inner connection that exists between what is eternal, permanent and general in modern social democracy [socialism] and the eternal Word of God, which in Jesus became flesh."[4] Barth, in other words, grants that the significance of Jesus is eternal, but he retorts that this is precisely what Jesus shares in common with socialism – not what makes the two different.

Barth next turns to the socialist objections. He anticipates their skepticism about his basic intentions. Is Barth only trying to use socialism in order to bring the politically minded into the fold of the church or to convert them to a Christin worldview? Here the worry is that Barth is actually a conservative dressed in socialist clothing. Barth's response to this set of objections is equally forceful. He clarifies that the connection between Jesus and socialism has nothing whatsoever to do with one's attitude toward the church. What Barth really wants is for his readers to have a "personal inner relation" with

---

4 Barth, "Jesus Christ and the Movement for Social Justice," 100.

this man Jesus. The church is only supposed to help people toward that end (though, Barth admits, it frequently gets in the way of it). In fact, the church is only a means to achieving a relation with Jesus. It is not, strictly speaking, necessary: "[A]t all times there have been people who have managed without [the church's] help." In short, Barth writes, "The church is not Jesus, and Jesus is not the church."[5] By drawing a sharp distinction between Jesus and the church, he assures his socialist listeners that they can devote themselves to the former without necessarily affiliating with the latter.

Similarly, Jesus does not bring ideas, but a "way of life." Barth is not at all concerned to bring his socialist friends to believe this or that Christian dogma. One can hold to all the correct Christian doctrines and still be "a complete heathen." Conversely, "as an atheist, a materialist, and a Darwinist, one can be a genuine follower and disciple of Jesus. Jesus is not the Christian world view and the Christian world view is not Jesus." Once again, having drawn a sharp distinction between Jesus and a Christian belief system, socialists may concern themselves with the former without having to concern themselves with the latter.

With these objections behind him, Barth dives into the subject matter itself. He argues that socialism and Jesus (when seen from the human side) are both movements "from below to above." Socialism is a movement of the economically dependent (i.e., the proletariat) to achieve economic independence – with all of the external, moral, and cultural consequences that will necessarily result. In the same way, Jesus himself was poor, and his disciples were all from the lowest rungs of society. As Barth observes, "One cannot reach lower down the social scale in the choice of one's associates than Jesus did."[6] Crucially, Jesus preached that the kingdom of God has come to the poor.

The common (though misguided) objection that both Christianity's cultured defenders and despisers frequently put forward is that the "kingdom of God" Jesus proclaimed is radically different from social democracy's vision of society. Whereas Jesus's kingdom of God preaches spirituality and inwardness, calls for personal conversion, and orients human beings toward a transcendent and heavenly realm, social democracy seeks revolution within an earthly, immanent realm.

---

5   Barth, "Jesus Christ and the Movement for Social Justice," 101.
6   Barth, "Jesus Christ and the Movement for Social Justice," 103.

Yet Barth responds that such oppositions have brought about "the great, momentous apostasy of the Christian church, her apostasy from Christ."[7] The church has accepted social misery as an accomplished fact in order to talk about spirit, cultivate the inner life, and prepare candidates for the hereafter. Jesus, on the contrary, completely overturns such oppositions: there are not two worlds – one transcendent, the other immanent; one heavenly, the other earthly – but the one reality of the kingdom of God. God is not opposed to the earth, but rather to evil. Redemption is not the process by which human beings leave the earth, but God's coming down to the earth: the Word becoming flesh.

For Jesus, the spirit is of course within the human person. Yet the spirit, if it is really the spirit of Jesus, necessarily strives to obtain dominion over that which is external, i.e., over actual life. God's will be done *on earth* as it is in heaven. Therefore, seen from the divine side, the gospel of Jesus is also a movement from above to below, from heaven to earth. The marks of this spirit's work are social help, reflected in the various healings of Jesus; opposition to material misery in word and deed; and the creation of new people who are striving to create a new world.

While Barth grants that Jesus obviously has nothing direct to say about the capitalist economic system or the socialist counter-theory, Barth thinks that Jesus does say a great deal about the issue of private property, from which one can infer his attitude toward these economic systems. When one studies Jesus's life and ministry, one notices that he is "more socialist than the socialists."[8] The church, which is essentially bourgeois on the issue of private property, has failed to appreciate Jesus's teaching against self-seeking mine versus thine. The church has failed to recognize that Jesus's gospel, if taken seriously, calls for the abolition of private property and the common ownership of the means of production.

Furthermore, the gospel calls human beings to be preoccupied not with their own individual eternal life, but with their solidarity with and for others. The cross of Jesus is the ultimate demonstration of giving up one's life for others. All of this finds a clear and pure expression, Barth thinks, in social democracy's idea of organization and comradeship. Jesus' spirit is one with the goals of socialism. Therefore, Christians who wish to follow Jesus should obey Jesus and participate in the movement for social justice today. And so-

---

7   Barth, "Jesus Christ and the Movement for Social Justice," 105.
8   Barth, "Jesus Christ and the Movement for Social Justice," 108.

cialists who are skeptical of Jesus should see in this man what it means to be a true socialist, i.e., how to pursue social justice.

For the young Barth, then, what matters is ultimately not the church, but Jesus. And what Jesus calls his disciples to is not a "religious" or "churchly" way of life or to a "Christian" worldview, but to a commitment – in word and deed – to the movement for social justice. In 1911, Barth believed that such a movement was most concretely embodied in the social democracy of his day, i.e., in the pursuit of political and economic solidarity, in the abolition of private property, and in the common ownership of the means of production. In all such things, the spirit of Jesus is most clearly and purely detected: "I find something of this power of God in social democracy's idea of organization. I also find it elsewhere, but here I find it more clearly and purely, and here I find it in the way in which it must be worked out in *our* time."[9] The church, when it does not get in the way of this spirit, is of only instrumental significance: it either helps one encounter the active spirit of Jesus in the present (i.e., in the movement for social justice) or it does not. What matters, for Barth, is active political organization in the spirit of Jesus: the two are in fact the same. Jesus, who "goes from century to century in ever-new revelations of his glory," has appeared in the present hour of history within the movement for social justice incarnated within socialism.[10]

"The Christian in Society" (1919)

Roughly eight years later, Barth was invited to give an address at the Conference on Religion and Social Relations (*die religiös-soziale Konferenz*) held in Tambach, Germany in September, 1919. Barth opens his lecture by claiming that the very thought of the Christian's place in society "fills us with hope but at the same time leaves us strangely unsettled."[11] On the one hand, this thought fills him with hope because society is not left wholly to itself. Every domain (the family, the economic order, art, science, the state, and so on) is modified by another factor that is full of promise: *the Christian*. But what is the Christian? "*[T]he Christian*" cannot mean "*the Christians*" – neither the mass of the baptized nor somehow the elect little company of religious socialists, nor even the most noble and pious Christians of whom we might

---

9   Barth, "Jesus Christ and the Movement for Social Justice," 113.
10 Barth, "Jesus Christ and the Movement for Social Justice," 114.
11 Karl Barth, "The Christian in Society," in *The Word of God and Theology*, ed. and trans. Amy Marga (London: Bloomsbury Publishing, 2011), 35.

otherwise think."[12] Rather, the Christian is "*the Christ*. The Christian is that which dwells in us. It is not us but is, rather, Christ in us [...]. 'In us' means 'above us,' 'behind us,' 'beyond us.'"[13] And yet, on the other hand, the thought of the Christian's place in society also fills him with questioning: Is Christ in human beings? Is he really in present-day society? Is Christ really *here*? Of course, he is. But in what sense? Where is he to be found? And how does his presence work in our midst? With these questions, Barth launches into a set of theological investigations that proceed along rather different lines than those taken in his earlier lecture on Jesus and socialism.

For the Barth at Tambach, these two magnitudes – *the Christian* and *society* – stand in paradoxical tension with one another. Does not the notion of *the Christian* inevitably suggest a holy domain set apart by itself? Is it really possible, as some would like to think, to simply open the sluices of the "Christ in us" and let the ready water stream over the thirsty land of society? Barth is unconvinced. "Readily available are the combinations like 'Christian-Social,' 'Evangelical-Social,' 'Religious-Social,' but it is well worth considering whether the hyphens we boldly draw are not dangerous short-circuits."[14] What was once axiomatic for Barth – the conviction that Jesus and a particular social movement (i.e., social democracy) are one and the same – has now become quite problematic. The question of this current essay is: what has changed for Barth at this point? And how do these changes affect his view of church and state?

Barth writes about God as follows: "The divine is something complete in itself, self-contained, new in kind, different from the world. It does not allow itself to be divided and distributed [...]. It wants to tear down and build up. It is complete in itself or it is nothing at all."[15] How then did humanity ever come to believe that the world of God has any available connection with human social life? How could human beings be so presumptuous as to think it does? As Barth writes,

> "To be sure, we may succeed in *secularizing* Christ for the umpteenth time – today (for example) for the sake of social democracy, pacifism, the Christian Youth Movement (*Wandervogel*), just as it was in the past for the sake of our fatherlands, for being Swiss and German, and for the sake of liberalism and the

---

12 Barth, "The Christian in Society," 36.
13 Barth, "The Christian in Society," 36.
14 Barth, "The Christian in Society," 37.
15 Barth, "The Christian in Society," 38.

educated classes. But are we not horrified by such a prospect? We do not want to betray Christ yet again."[16]

Barth now thinks that those who would relate Christ to society are in a rather perplexing situation. Human beings need Christ in society, but they do not know how to bring him into it. Barth notes, "How difficult it is to take even the smallest steps with Christ in society with a pure heart and reverence for the holy! With what brittleness does the divine – if it is the divine – relate to the human, which we so gladly want to mix together today!"[17] Society today is a whole in itself and autonomous from God in many respects. Human beings may try to reverse such secularizing trends by re-clericalizing society, as some are evidently trying to do. But Barth thinks that putting new patches on an old garment does not make the old garment new. He is skeptical about all such efforts, which he dismisses as temptations to "modern ecclesiasticism." Human beings would be more honest to confess that "We cannot, therefore, in accordance with the old admonition, reckon soberly enough with 'reality' if we are to confront the task of carrying out our program. If things stay as they are, it is with good reason that there are impossible ideals and unreachable goals."[18] There is no straightforward way to bring Christ into society.

On the one hand, the thought of the Christian's place in society leaves one with a great promise; on the other hand, human beings are left perplexed by an unhappy separation between these two magnitudes. Both the promise and the perplexing separation must be kept in clear view. There is no solution; better, there is only one solution, and it is found in God. The task is not to resolve the tension, but rather to live amidst the tension in what Barth describes as a "priestly awakening."[19] Such a posture partakes in *God's* movement in history. This movement is not identical with the socialistic movement or with a religious Christian movement. Instead, this is a movement from above that transcends such movements and yet penetrates them at the same time. The movement of God in history is revealed in the resurrection of Jesus Christ from the dead.

What the resurrection demonstrates is that Christ is the absolutely new revelation from above. In him, humanity stands in immediate relation to

---

16   Barth, "The Christian in Society," 38.
17   Barth, "The Christian in Society," 38.
18   Barth, "The Christian in Society," 41.
19   Barth, "The Christian in Society," 41.

God; new life breaks in upon humanity from a third dimension. Those who participate in this movement are given a wholly new motivation. Because human beings now stand in an immediate relation to God, no human independence from God is ultimate. Rather, the soul that has been awakened to its immediacy to God is compelled to issue a categorical challenge to all alleged authorities in life, testing them by *the* authority of God:

> "We can no longer allow ourselves to be *completely* deceived as to the true character of the powers of death by the ideologies with which they surround themselves and by everything that speaks only relatively for their validity. There is something in us that calls them into question from the ground up."[20]

In this way, Barth issues a relative justification for the various movements of his day that attack the authority of family for its own sake, art for its own sake, work for its own sake, religion for its own sake, and so on. "We want to comprehend our contemporaries, from Naumann to Blumhardt, from Wilson, to Lenin, in all the various stages of the same movement in which we see them. We want to comprehend our time and its signs, to comprehend ourselves in our strange unrest and turbulence."[21] Barth is able to look upon such critiques of the social order with sympathy and understanding.

And yet, Barth also urges that human beings must not limit their conception of the kingdom of God to reform movements and social revolutions. While protest against a particular social order is an "integral moment" in the kingdom of God, humanity must not forget that "The kingdom of God does not begin with our protest movements. It is a revolution that *precedes* every other, just as it *precedes* everything that exists."[22] What comes before all human social criticism and every human revolutionary movement is the original synthesis that all things were created by Christ and for Christ. The human negation of the world is tempered by an affirmation of the world as God's possession in Christ. The creator remains the creator even of the fallen world and of the sinful human social order:

> "To find ourselves in God means to affirm him in the world as it is, and not in some transcendental dream world. The genuine and radical denial that we intend in our protest movements can grow only out of this affirmation. The true

---

20 Barth, "The Christian in Society," 47.
21 Barth, "The Christian in Society," 49.
22 Barth, "The Christian in Society," 52.

antithesis can only grow out of the thesis. The true – that is, the original – antithesis grows out of the synthesis."[23]

In humanity's very opposition to the social order, they are reminded that the social order is still God's: "The recognition of the *absolute vanity* of life under the sun, of existence in light of the life of God above the heavens, gives rise to the knowledge of the *possibility* and *value* of this vain life, a possibility and value that are not completely irrelevant and futile, even if they are *relative*."[24] Human beings are therefore free to be "more romantic than the Romanticists" and "more humanistic than the Humanists."[25] They are to take up their appointed place in the world's march – freely going in and out of the house of publicans and sinners, of the state, of secular social democracy, and so on – without the fear of becoming servants of idols. Therefore, human beings are saved from a false denial of life (i.e., a kind of negation that turns negation into a theme in its own right).

Yet Barth is no less insistent that humanity is saved from a false affirmation of life. The antithesis, no less than the thesis, issues from the synthesis. He writes, "*We* live more deeply in the 'No' than in the 'Yes,' deeper in criticism and protest than in naivety, deeper in our yearning for the future than in our participation in the present."[26] There can be no question, then, of a kind of quietism that accepts the world as it is or waits for another world beyond: "We can no longer bring about rest through vague references to the realm beyond, for that 'other side' now unsettles us with its absence, with its knocking on the closed door of this present realm."[27] For Barth, this amounts to a kind of dynamic affirmation of society, followed by an ever-stronger denunciation of that same society.

Yet human beings must take care that neither their Yes nor their No is made into a theme by itself: "Our 'Yes,' like our 'No,' carries its limitations in itself. In so far as it is God who gives us our test – and a greater unrest – neither rest nor unrest can be our final viewpoint of the world, no matter how necessary each one is."[28] Both humanity's naïve acceptance and critical attitude can fall into right practical relation to each other only when human beings are attuned to God's working in history in the resurrection of Jesus

---

23   Barth, "The Christian in Society," 52.
24   Barth, "The Christian in Society," 53–54.
25   Barth, "The Christian in Society," 54.
26   Barth, "The Christian in Society," 60.
27   Barth, "The Christian in Society," 63.
28   Barth, "The Christian in Society," 65.

Christ, which is both the affirmation of the world as God's world and the negation of the fallen world as standing in need of God's salvific redemption. Thesis and antithesis are united only in the synthesis that is in God alone. As Barth writes, "For, what can the Christin in society do except follow closely that which is done by *God*?"[29] Oriented toward God, the Christian will be in a position to utter the affirmation and negation that issue from the divine synthesis.

In sum, Barth's conception of church and state in this lecture has changed. Whereas before, Jesus and the movement for social justice (i.e., the service of God and the service of humanity) were thought to be identical, here one can see Barth struggling to relate these two magnitudes that stand in a paradoxical tension with one another. The movement of God in history, a movement that is defined by the resurrection of Jesus Christ, simultaneously affirms the world as it is (i.e., as a world created by God) and negates that world as in need of salvation (i.e., as a world God redeems). The human thesis and antithesis are both grounded and negated by the original synthesis in God. This synthesis, crucially, neither collapses the thesis into the antithesis nor the antithesis into the thesis.

Rather, this synthesis places the thesis and the antithesis, the affirmation and the negation, within the movement of God in history. Both church and state thus seem to be given their relative justification and ultimate negation: human beings are freed by the original synthesis to freely go in and out of both church and state, affirming and negating both on the basis of the prior movement of God in Christ. In any case, social democracy is not the sole, or even the privileged, instantiation of Jesus in history. Social democracy is as much subjected to the divine affirmation and negation as the church. Humanity participates in both as those who have been awakened to the divine revolution that comes from beyond history, by which all human ordinances in church and state have been dissolved. Humanity's job is not to dissolve them in the present, but to submit to the dissolution that comes from God alone. In the meantime, human beings are but priestly agitators who, because they know that church and state are under God's ultimate judgment, can treat them with the seriousness – and also the detached realism – with which they are due in the time that remains.

---

29 Barth, "The Christian in Society," 69.

"The Christian Community and the Civil Community" (1946)

In this third address, "The Christian Community and the Civil Community" (1946), the reader encounters yet another conception of church/state relations. The position articulated here is not without precedent in Barth's thought. In fact, in many ways, Barth's writing in this third address is a further elaboration upon a position he began to articulate in an earlier essay, "Church and State" (*Rechtfertigung und Recht*, 1938). This later essay will be examined because it contains the clearest description of Barth's mature political theological outlook.

In this essay, Barth claims that the Christian community is conscious of the need for the existence of the civil community in the still unredeemed world. In this fallen world, humans have the need for "kings." They need to be subject to an external, relative, and provisional order of law, defended by a superior authority and force. Without the civil community, there would only be chaos. As Barth writes, "[The Christian community] sees as the visible means of this protection of human life from chaos the existence of the civil community."[30] The church, which enjoys the protection afforded by the state and thanks God for this protection, "knows that without this political order there would be no Christian order." Regardless of whether state officials are Christians, the civil community is a divine *ordinatio* or *exousia* in accordance with the will of God (Rom. 13:1). The state is not a product of sin, but rather it is an instrument and order of divine grace. The state is the visible sign that humanity has not been forsaken but is being preserved and sustained by God. The state also protects humanity from the invasion of chaos by giving humanity "time for the preaching of the gospel; time for repentance; time for faith."[31] In this way, the state performs a definite service to the divine providence and plan of salvation. The state is not separate from the kingdom of Jesus Christ; its foundations and influence are not autonomous: "It is outside the Church but not outside the range of Christ's dominion – it is an exponent of His kingdom." The church, therefore, acknowledges the benefaction of this divine ordinance with thankful and reverent hearts. There can be no non-political Christianity and no Christianity that is indifferent to politics. The church is not allowed to be indifferent or neutral towards the state.

---

30 Karl Barth, "The Christian Community and the Civil Community," in *Community, State, and Church: Three Essays* (Eugene, OR: Wipf & Stock, 2004), 155.
31 Barth, "The Christian Community and the Civil Community," 156.

And yet, the church must not lose sight of its own unique task, a task that the state cannot take away from it. The church proclaims the rule of Jesus Christ and the hope of the kingdom of God. The church knows itself to be the inner circle of the kingdom of God, whereas the state is the outer circle. The church believes in and preaches Jesus Christ, who is Lord of the church and of the whole world. With an awareness of its particular task, the church does not stop at the boundary where the inner and outer circles meet, but rather pursues faith, hope, and love on both sides of the boundary.

In the sphere of the civil community, the Christian community shares common interests with the world and gives practical expression to this community of interests. In this way, the church subordinates itself to the cause of the state: "Christians should carry out what is required of them for the establishment, preservation, and maintenance of the civil community and for the execution of its task, because, although they are Christians and, as such, have their home elsewhere, they also live in this outer circle."[32] This means that the church is not allowed to be indifferent to particular political patterns and realities. The church must take responsibility for the shape and reality of the civil community by "distinguishing between the just and the unjust State, that is between the better and the worse political form and reality; between order and caprice; between government and tyranny; between freedom and anarchy; between community and collectivism; between personal rights and individualism; between the State as described in Romans 13 and the State as described in Revelation 13."[33]

Since members of the church are simultaneously members of the state, Christians ought to be servants of the civil community out of obedience to God. This means that Christians should help the state fulfill its divine ordinance by establishing a correspondence between the will of God in Jesus Christ and human social institutions. The church, in other words, must see to it that human politics and the politics of God proceed on parallel lines.

The notion of the church's political activism raises a crucial question: What is the proper norm of Christian decision-making in the civil sphere? If Christians are going to make political decisions, they need to be guided by some principle. Many political norms are readily available to humanity: How about the very ancient principle, "To each their own"? Or the utilitarian formula, "The greatest happiness of the greatest number"? Or the Marxist

---

32 Barth, "The Christian Community and the Civil Community," 159.
33 Barth, "The Christian Community and the Civil Community," 162.

slogan, "From each according to his ability, to each according to his needs!"? Or the Leninist motto, "He who does not work shall not eat"? Or even the libertarian motto, "Taxation is theft!" Whatever humanity might think of these and various other political principles, Barth is adamant that the church's political decision-making should be guided not by natural law, or some ideological system, or a political program, but by human knowledge of the gospel and the kingdom of God.

In other words, according to the mature Barth, Christians should be anchored in theological commitments and then make political decisions that are consonant with those commitments. He describes this as the church's striving to mold the state into an allegory of the kingdom of God. Along these lines, Barth makes a series of rather suggestive arguments about the political consequences of various Christian doctrines – each doctrine serving as a sort of ad hoc political norm. For example, Barth argues that because God became human in Jesus Christ, Christians should be committed to concrete human beings rather than to some abstract idea such as the Nation, the GDP, or Progress; because God in Christ justifies human beings, Christians should be committed to constitutional government, to civil liberties and rights, and to equal protection under the law; because Jesus came to seek and save the lost, Christians should be committed to social justice and the preferential option for the poor; because there are a variety of spiritual gifts within the church, Christians should be committed to the separation of executive, legislative, and judicial powers in secular government; because God chose human words to be the vehicle of the free Word of God, Christians should be committed to freedom of speech, freedom of the press, and so on. In this way, Barth shows how a commitment to the gospel and the kingdom of God can and should be given expression in secular politics.

The Christian community acts within the meaning and limits of its own mission and competence when it speaks to important situations in the political life of secular polities (e.g., by making representations to the authorities, by public proclamations, by Christian journalism, etc.). The church "will be careful to select, as wisely as possible, the particular political situations in which it deems it right to speak, and it will have to choose its words very prudently and very definitely if it is to be heard."[34] Yet Barth is clear that when applying Christian convictions to the political sphere, the Christian community should draw its attention to the gospel only *indirectly*, i.e., as reflected

---

34 Barth, "The Christian Community and the Civil Community," 185.

in its political decisions. The church should therefore make its political decisions intelligible and victorious not on account of their Christian premises but simply for the reason that "they are politically better and more calculated to preserve and develop the common life."[35] Christians must therefore bring their Christianity into the political sphere anonymously, proposing political decisions that could be the decisions of "any other citizens" (regardless of their religious profession or lack thereof).

In sum, the framework for church/state relations articulated in this mature essay construes both of these institutions as playing important, though clearly distinct, roles in the divine economy of salvation. The church is the inner circle of God's kingdom, and the state is the outer circle. Christians are aware of the final end of all things in Christ, and with this knowledge they work on behalf of the secular state, which performs a definite service to the world in the time that remains. Though the just state is not identical with any one particular political form, the church is to participate in the various tasks of daily politics in its effort to help the state fulfill its God-given ordinance. Crucially, this will require that Christians draw upon their Christian convictions in order to be servants of the state. The state, meanwhile, is called upon to protect the church's right to proclaim the gospel and the kingdom of God.

Conclusion

Barth's political theology offers us a range of ways to think about the relation between church and state in the life of the Christian. From his early identification of the spirit of Jesus with the movement for social justice as embodied in social democracy; to his paradoxical juxtaposition of church and state as simultaneously affirmed and radically negated by the judgment of God in Jesus Christ from above; to his state-supporting and politically-engaged Christian confessionalism – each offers a rich storehouse of ways to think about the tasks of Christian faith in the political domain.

One would be wise to resist the temptation to pick one of the above orientations as the properly "Barthian" one. Each of them, in its own way, shares important continuities with Barth's theology. And yet, there are noticeable differences between them. What they all share in common, however, is a serious commitment to the life of politics. There is never a question, for Barth, at *any* stage of his political theology, of whether a Christian should turn away

---

35   Barth, "The Christian Community and the Civil Community," 183.

from the political sphere. Barth's conception of Christian faith and churchly existence is always politically-engaged. Additionally, Barth's various approaches to church and state all share a resolute commitment to politics *as politics*. Barth makes no attempt to commandeer the political domain for explicitly Christian purposes. Rather, for him, the church is always a servant – first and foremost of God, but also in practice of the state. Christians must not raise attention to themselves, so much as be of service to the common good. In this way, the God who is above both church and state is honored.

Barth's various approaches to church and state, whatever their noticeable differences, are rather different from many of the visions put forward in our own day. On the one hand, some have attempted to turn Christians away from society at large and the domain of secular politics specifically. One might think, for instance, of those who are calling for a "benedict option" as a strategy for Christians who feel they are losing the culture wars.[36] On the other hand, there are some who seek to enforce explicitly Christian norms within the domain of politics. One can detect this trend today in forms of Protestant Christian nationalism and Roman Catholic integralism.[37]

By contrast, Barth's political theological construals of church/state relations can provide a more helpful way to think about the civic responsibilities of Christians. From Barth's perspective, there can be no Christian turning away from secular politics. The church should carry out what is required of it for "the establishment, preservation, and maintenance of the civil community and for the execution of its task."[38] This will of course require that individual Christians, scattered abroad as citizens of various states, participate in the manifold activities associated with civic life in the secular polities in which they find themselves – party politics, journalism and media, campaigning and voting, organizing and protesting. Christians can do all of this with a sense of honest realism about the limits of politics in a fallen world, but also with a sense of heartfelt conviction that the civil cause, and not just the Christian cause, is the cause of the one God.

Conversely, Barth would of course confess that Jesus Christ is Lord over the state and that the state, as an instrument of God, is responsible to this

---

36 Cf. Rod Dreher, *The Benedict Option: A Strategy for Christians in a Post-Christian Nation* (New York: Sentinel, 2017).
37 Cf. Stephen Wolfe, *The Case for Christian Nationalism* (Moscow, Idaho: Canon Press, 2022); Kevin Vallier, *All the Kingdoms of the World: On Radical Religious Alternatives to Liberalism* (New York: Oxford University Press, 2023).
38 Barth, "The Christian Community and the Civil Community," 159.

Lord who is its (hidden) center. However, Barth would strongly insist that the respective roles of the church and the state in the divine economy of salvation must be differentiated clearly. Rather than allow the church to be the church and the state to be the state, the vision espoused by Christian nationalism, for example, espouses a vision that encourages the church to fight for power and public recognition in the political sphere and the state to subordinate itself to the goals of the church. Christian nationalism fails to understand that the state need not become "Christian" in order to fulfill the will of God for which it was created, and Christians need not bring their explicit theological commitments into the political domain in order to fulfill their God-given civic responsibilities.

Barth's political theology, as already discussed, insists that the state is in fact called upon by God to be secular – to fulfill its divine ordinance using worldly, profane means. The state fulfills God's will not by becoming a "Christian" state or by giving Christians special treatment, but by achieving an external, relative, and provisional humanization of existence according to the measure of human insight and capacity. Meanwhile, Christians fulfill their civic responsibilities not by making the state more "Christian," but by inconspicuously letting their theological convictions shape and inform their political decisions – for the benefit not merely of Christians but for the common good.

In precisely this spirit, Barth's political theology, across its various iterations, encourages Christians to reason about politics *as* Christians and then translate and indirectly apply those theological reasonings to the domain of secular politics. I have sketched how Barth's construal of church/state relations improves upon some of the increasingly popular alternatives today. Barth's alternative to Christian separatism, nationalism, and integralism encourages Christians to indirectly apply their theological commitments to their political decision-making out of a desire to help all members of the civil community lead lives that are consonant with the supreme Lordship and grace of God in Jesus Christ.

Joe Kauslick

Negation and Affirmation, Judgment, and Grace

Karl Barth's *The Christian Life* as a Theology of Christian Accountability

Introduction

In this article, I will provide a reading of Barth's account of the Christian life in terms of accountability.[1] I will first give a definition and brief explanation of the concept in general. Then I will apply the concept to Barth's conception of the Christian life. My focus within Barth's account will be on the authority and significance of the coming of God's Kingdom through Jesus' fulfillment of the broken covenant, and the dialectical situation within which the Christian life is led. The analysis yields some surprising results, results which have

---

1   Accountability has only very recently received direct scholarly attention in Christian theology and ethics, and only from one major research project. See C. Stephen Evans, *Living Accountably: Accountability as a Virtue* (New York: Oxford University Press, 2023); Andrew B. Torrance, *Accountability to God* (New York: Oxford University Press, 2023); Brendan Case, *The Accountable Animal: Justice, Justification, and Judgment* (New York: Bloomsbury Academic, 2021). See also the journal articles in psychology that developed out of the Living Accountably Project: Charlotte V.O. Witvliet et al., "Transcendent Accountability: Construct and Measurement of a Virtue That Connects Religion, Spirituality, and Positive Psychology," *The Journal of Positive Psychology* (February 26, 2023): 1–14; John R. Peteet, Charlotte V. O. Witvliet, and C. Stephen Evans, "Accountability as a Key Virtue in Mental Health and Human Flourishing," *Philosophy, Psychiatry, & Psychology* 29, no. 1 (2022): 49–60; John R. Peteet, Charlotte V. O. Witvliet, and C. Stephen Evans, "Accountability and Autonomy," *Philosophy, Psychiatry, & Psychology* 29, no. 1 (2022): 69–71; Matt Bradshaw et al., "Perceptions of Accountability to God and Psychological Well-Being Among US Adults," *Journal of Religion and Health* 61, no. 1 (February 1, 2022): 327–52; and Charlotte V. O. Witvliet et al., "Apology and Restitution: The Psychophysiology of Forgiveness After Accountable Relational Repair Responses," *Frontiers in Psychology* 11 (2020).

significant implications for accountability more generally even for those who do not share or endorse the Barthian Christian commitments on which they were developed.

The Christian Life

For God to be the God and Father of our Lord Jesus Christ entails that God has determined to be in covenant with humanity through Jesus.[2] For that covenant to obtain, there must be a covenant partner who is the recipient of God's grace, the beneficiary of God's election. The very fact that God is the one in whom humanity and all of creation lives, moves, and has its being (Acts 17:28), that God is Jesus Christ, in whom all things cohere and who is fully human and fully divine, humanity is made a covenant partner with God. And as that covenant partner, the Lord of the covenant commands the subjects of the covenant, commanding them to free and responsible obedience.[3] "It is in and with man's determination by God as this takes place in predestination that the question arises of man's self-determination, his responsibility and decision, his obedience and action."[4] For Barth, then, to be committed to the claim that Jesus is the revelation of God entails (at first implicitly, then made explicit) the claims about the covenant of grace, about God's election, about God's command, God's determination of humanity and the consequent ethical question of the human being's obedience. The logic from the doctrine of *God* to the doctrine of *God's command* to the question

---

2   See Karl Barth, *Church Dogmatics, Volume II: The Doctrine of God, Part 2*, ed. Geoffrey W. Bromiley and Thomas F. Torrance, trans. G. W. Bromiley et al. (Edinburgh: T&T Clark, 1957), 7. Hereafter *CD II/2*.
3   My view of Barth's theological ethics comports with Paul T. Nimmo, *Being in Action: The Theological Shape of Barth's Ethical Vision* (New York: T&T Clark, 2007) and Gerald P. McKenny, *The Analogy of Grace: Karl Barth's Moral Theology* (New York: Oxford University Press, 2010); *Karl Barth's Moral Thought*, Oxford Studies in Theological Ethics (Oxford: Oxford University Press, 2021). Their positions are not identical, of course, but for my purposes here, their views accord with mine. Nevertheless, McKenny's conclusion against the utility of Barth's central theological ethical claim that Jesus is the norm of human action is one that I do not agree with – though that is an argument to explore on another occasion.
4   Barth, *CD II/2*, 511.

of human obedience is also the avenue through which Barth argues that God has made Godself "originally responsible" for humanity.[5]

> "The fact that [God] gives man His command, that He subjects man to his command, means that He makes Himself responsible not only for its authority but also for its fulfillment [...] the matter of theological ethics is the responsibility which God has assumed for us in the fact the He has made us accountable through his command."[6]

God's own self-determination and commitment to and for humanity constitutes the human being as responsible. Entailed in God's commanding of the human covenant partner is God's taking and treating them as having the authority and responsibility to be the covenant partner who can and will hear and heed God's command. And God's own responsibility here is the commitment to be the Commanding God who constitutes the covenant partner as one who obeys. But further still, since God in Jesus Christ is that obedient covenant partner who is the "author and finisher" of our own reconciled partnership with God, God is also responsible and accountable as *the* human covenant partner.

Barth's ethics of reconciliation provides the resources for an account of how Christians are accountable to themselves, the church, and the world as they live the Christian life. In his unfinished ethics of reconciliation, Barth draws out the implications of one his basic theological ethical claims: that God makes Godself originally responsible for humanity in and through God's command. In terms of the doctrine of reconciliation, Christians are made responsible by God's act as reconciler. Christians reckon with the knowledge and ignorance of God and the hallowing and desecration of God's name in all spheres of life (world, church community, themselves). Christians are aware of, recognize, acknowledge, and suffer under the above situation in themselves first and foremost, then the church, then the world. And finally, Christians engage in conflict with and revolt against ignorance and desecration of God for the sake of all humanity.

For the structure and development of this special ethic, Barth determines that invocation is the central theme to be developed for the Christian life. "What God permits man, what he expects, wills, and requires of him, is a

---

5   This claim first appears as part of the first main thesis of the chapter on God's command in Barth's doctrine of God, *CD* II/2, 509.
6   Barth, *CD II/2*, 543.

Negation and Affirmation, Judgment, and Grace 99

life of calling upon him."[7] Thus, the Christian life is developed with reference to the Lord's prayer. The invocations of that prayer structure the exposition of the ethic. The ethics of reconciliation has its own special definition of the ethical problem faced by those who stand under God's judgment and forgiveness in Jesus Christ.[8] Like all theology for Barth, the Word of God revealed in the divine-human union of the person and work of Jesus provides the question and the answer of ethics. "[T]he human action is good which is commanded by God in his Word and is obedient to him."[9] Ethics has to do "with [the command of God's] significance and outworking in the life of the man to whom it comes, with the freedom for good action which is demanded of him but also granted, granted to him but also demanded, as God commands him."[10] This first stipulation is consistent with the dialectics of the *Römerbrief*, which begins with God and assesses human life and conduct by the standard of the Word of God. Hence, human beings need to be granted the very capacity to obey the command of God even as God demands their obedience (in fact, this demand for obedience is what creates the capacity for such obedience). Invocation captures this need and the faith that God will meet it.

The character of the Christian in the invocation of this prayer is zeal for the honor of God. Zeal is Barth's term for the specific kind of suffering Christians experience in their unfulfilled desire for the hallowing of God's name; a desire which they seek to fulfill but that can only be fulfilled by God.[11] Barth unpacks the character of Christian zeal dialectically and geometrically. Geometrically, Barth envisions three concentric circles of the Christian life.[12] The circles are distinct from one another but also intimately related. The outermost circle is the world. The world is the whole of God's creation in its totality. For Barth's reflections on the dynamics of the Christian life, however, he delimits his understanding of the world. "We take the term 'world' to refer specifically to creation as the world of the man who shapes the wider sphere and who is thus responsible to its Creator for the way it is. The world, then, is the world as this man can to a large extent see and grasp and control it. It is

---

7   Karl Barth, *The Christian Life*, trans. Geoffrey William Bromiley, 2nd ed. (New York: Bloomsbury T&T Clark, 2017), 75.
8   Barth, *The Christian Life*, 19–20.
9   Barth, *The Christian Life*, 20.
10 Barth, *The Christian Life*, 20.
11 Barth, *The Christian Life*, 163–169.
12 Barth, *The Christian Life*, 170–218 and 257–285.

the human world."¹³ The middle circle is the church. The church is a "worldly entity" but is not identical with the world. The church "stands to the rest of the world in an independent and distinctively critical and positive relationship [...]. It is in the world as the people, the possession, and the sanctuary of God."¹⁴ The life of the individual Christian is the innermost circle. The conditions of the world and the church apply to the individual Christian in a personal way and in a way that refracts out to the church and the world.

Christian zeal also has a dialectical character operative in each sphere: God is both known and unknown. This dialectic of the known and unknown God is the situation about which Christians respond with zeal for and the invocation of God's holiness. It is applied to each of the three circles in terms of God being both known and unknown in the world, the church, and the individual Christian. Barth's discussion of the knowledge and ignorance of God in the church illustrates this dialectic. The church knows God in a way that is distinct from the world. "The church has its origin in the completed self-declaration of God."¹⁵ The church has heard God's Yes to the world and responded in and through Jesus with a corresponding Yes to God. And this double Yes transforms into the task and goal of the church in the world: to bear witness to God's and humanity's Yes.¹⁶ But this knowledge of God in the church, the knowledge that constitutes it, is paired with the paradoxical ignorance of God in the church.

The nature of this relationship between the church and the world is all the more clear when he returns to the question of how zeal for the honor of God bears itself out in Christian witness in and for the world.¹⁷ Barth first affirms that "the Christian is a child and citizen of the world."¹⁸ The Christian speaks a certain language, was brought up in a certain family, nation, and culture. And beyond this more generic sense of the world is the more theologically inflected version: the Christian is a child and citizen of fallen creation, creation that is ignorant of God, fails to acknowledge God, and rejects God. But insofar as the Christian is also a child of God – that is, *qua* Christian – there is an obligation to serve the world.

---

13   Barth, *The Christian Life*, 171.
14   Barth, *The Christian Life*, 192.
15   Barth, *The Christian Life*, 192.
16   Barth, *The Christian Life*, 192–194.
17   Barth, *The Christian Life*, 273–285.
18   Barth, *The Christian Life*, 273.

Christian activity in the world presupposes that life in the interior spheres is in order. If they are not, this will undermine the witness of the Christian. One might be tempted to think that having the interior spheres of the personal and the ecclesial in order asserts a sequential logic to Christian witness in the world. The Christian must have faith and zeal for God, the Church must be in submission to God in its petition to God. Ignorance of God and desecration of the name of God must be fully eradicated. Only then can the Christian or the church bear witness to the world. There is a sense in which this is true. The faith of the Christian and the Christian's invocation of God must be in place for there to be witness. But this is a constitutive claim rather than a sequential one. The existence of the interior spheres depends upon the faith and zeal of the Christian and the church. If these were not in place, there would be no Christian or church. But just as these conditions are constitutive, they are not fully established. The Christian and the church are not expected (nor able) to be perfectly faithful, perfectly zealous, perfectly righteous. This is not possible and is contrary to Barth's Lutheran understanding of the Christian and the church as simultaneously saint and sinner, righteous and unrighteous.[19] Furthermore, it is the very life of the Christian and the church that bears witness in and for the world. Witness is not a separate activity cordoned off from other activities, as if the church could bear witness or not in the same way that a person can run or not. Every activity of the Christian and the church *qua* Christian is itself witness – or at least potentially so – ripe for being taken and treated as such in and for the world.

The character of Christian witness in and for the world is thoroughly dialectical. It takes seriously the dialectical situation of the presence of knowledge and ignorance of God in the church and the world. Failure to do so results in similar extremes as the church in excess and the church in defect. Witness conducted as outright and total negation renders impossible the task of the Christian to resist, call out, and correct the rebellion of the world against its knowledge of God. Such negation can take the form of a quasi-monastic retreat whereby an alternative Christian "world" is created apart from the world. Or it takes the form of Christian crusade: acts that defend the Christian viewpoint against alternatives and/or that attack the alternative positions in the world and expose their origins in the ignorance of God.[20]

---

[19] Of course, Barth has his own take on the Lutheran concept of *simul justus et peccator* so the uses are not equivalent.
[20] Barth, *The Christian Life*, 277–278.

"Either way the aim is to do injury to the worldliness of the world, to woo and win those who are outside for the gospel of God, and thus to chase away the darkness by the light."[21] By contrast, in outright affirmation, Christians enter into the world and adapt to it and change it from within. For although the world opposes God, it is already reconciled to God, after all.

Both of forms of one-sidedness fail to account for the dialectical situation of life in the world for Christians, overestimates either the knowledge or ignorance of God, and fails to distinguish between human and divine action. Exclusively negative witness underestimates the existing knowledge of God in the world that makes complete separation and alienation impossible. Moreover, it overestimates the Christian ability to negate given the Christian's own worldliness and thus also omits the affirmative content of Christian witness to the world. In sum, outright negation loses the necessary humility and modesty of Christian witness.[22] On the other hand, affirmative witness naively assumes that the world's opposition to God is not too severe, that the world is able to overcome its opposition through the work of the Christian. But the Christian is forced to conceal their transformative agenda to infiltrate the world. This forces the Christian hide the very thing that needs to be revealed (the Word of God) to effect the world's transformation. Additionally, the one-sided affirmation of the gospel is meaningless without the negation that is necessarily hidden and obscured by that one-sidedness. Thus, outright affirmation fails to have the courage of obedience, resolution, and nonconformity.[23]

For Barth, the difference between God and creatures makes all the difference for Christian knowledge of and witness to revelation. But this does not mean that discontinuity and radical breaking is all to the story. For one thing, God's very being and action is to be one who loves in freedom. This means that God loves us and wants to be with us in the closest possible fellowship. God wills that those who are not God would share in God's very own love and life. Here already in the nature of God is something like a simultaneous or mutually constitutive separation and connection between God and humanity. But this Barthian dialectic continues in God's effort to reconcile with humanity after fellowship has been broken and threatened with dissolution. God establishes covenant with Israel and thereby all humanity. This is the

---

21 Barth, *The Christian Life*, 278.
22 Barth, *The Christian Life*, 279.
23 Barth, *The Christian Life*, 281.

created mechanism of God's will for fellowship. But that covenant is broken through sin, which most fundamentally is rejection of – a radical break with – fellowship with God. Yet, God does not accept this break, this fissure. God rejects the rejection of humanity. Through the incarnate Son of God in Jesus, God humbles Godself and exalts humanity to establish reconciliation between them.

Here the complexity of discontinuity and continuity, of rejection and acceptance is important. God set out to have fellowship with humanity (connection). Humanity rejects this fellowship (disconnection). God rejects the rejection of humanity (discontinuity) and instead fulfills the broken covenant (continuity) in the reconciling work of Jesus. This dialectic of reconciliation continues in its ethical effects on the Christian, the Christian community, and their witness in and for the world. In the life of the Christian, in the Christian community, and in the world, the Christian experiences God being known and unknown, of God's name being hallowed and being desecrated. This combination is constant and simultaneous at every level of relationship. (Recall that Barth uses the image of concentric circles.) Thus, neither wholesale acceptance nor wholesale rejection at each layer is an acceptable response of one who is reconciled to God. And this is least of all in the world.

Christian witness cannot take only the form of negation or affirmation of the world; instead, Christian witness *at times* will be affirmation of the world, *at others* negation.[24]

What determines a particular act of witness as negation or affirmation is not so much the needs of the situation or context, but the determination of the Word of God. Here Barth's emphasis of God's command as event and not legalism or casuistry expresses itself anew. For the church or a Christian 1) to habitually or by default criticize or resist the world because of the world's ignorance and desecration of God in the world alone, or 2) to parrot, support or affirm the world because it has already been reconciled to God in Christ, are two opposite expressions of the same theological and ethical mistake:

---

24 "For all the secularity that he cannot peel off, [the Christian's] action in the world will be a spiritual one, since its concern will be neither with basic opposition to the world nor basic agreement with it, but only with ever new attention to the free and living Word of his Lord as the head of the community that he has chosen and called and also as Lord of the world […]. No matter whether he has now to negate the world or now to affirm it, whether he has now to be somewhat alien to it now or now to be somewhat in conformity with it, with courage and humility he has to be a witness of this Word to the world" (Barth, *The Christian Life*, 281–282).

taking God's command as a perspicuous and universal law which is to be followed at all times in all circumstances.[25]

What distinguishes the Christian in the world is that, unlike the world, the Christian has *understood and responded to the Word* in the world.

> "To be a witness – this means that among all other men of the world he has to think and speak and act as himself a man of the world who in distinction from the rest has heard the Word and recognized the value that it has for him in this outermost circle of his existence too, the authority which it claims here, and the promise which is pronounces here."[26]

Yet the Christian's witness of the Word to the world is *not* to conquer and transform the world. This is God's prerogative and action, not the Christian's. What they must do instead is live in the world in such a way that their way of life becomes like a text of the Word.[27] The Word so shapes their choices, desires, and actions in the world that their lives are demonstrations of the Word. This text is not only for Christians, but for non-Christians as well. Non-Christians may not be able to read or understand the text of the Christian's life, but that is not a requirement. Instead, the Christian's life should be so shaped by the Word that there is a text to be read, even if it is not understood.

Importantly, the text is not only explicitly discursive, but first and foremost performative. "What is to be expected of Christians is simply but undeniably this. In what they do or leave undone they make themselves known to the world as understanding hearers of the Word and thus draw attention to the Word in their existence."[28] The Christian is to be a doer of the Word first and foremost, though explanation and commentary may be required from time to time. That these actions bear fruit and are successful is, once again, not the goal and is only based on divine action.

---

25 It is not difficult to see the loudest voices of the right- and left-wing churches and Christians in the United States as mapping onto these extremes.
26 Barth, *The Christian Life*, 282.
27 Barth's comments here on Christian witness as text of the Word is what I take to be the best of what post-liberal theology offers with its Wittgensteinian inflection on language games and theology. See George A. Lindbeck, *The Nature of Doctrine: Religion and Theology in a Postliberal Age*, 25th anniversary ed. (Louisville, KY: Westminster John Knox Press, 2009) and especially Kathryn Tanner, *Theories of Culture: A New Agenda for Theology* (Minneapolis, MN: Fortress Press, 1997).
28 Barth, *The Christian Life*, 282.

The final section of *The Christian Life* shifts its attention from the first petition of the Lord's Prayer, that God's name be hallowed, to the second, that God's kingdom would come. Where the corresponding response from Christians who pray the first petition is zeal for the honor of God, in the second petition the corresponding action of Christians is the struggle for human righteousness. "Christians are summoned by God's command not only to zeal for God's honor but also to a simultaneous and related revolt, and therefore entry into a conflict."[29] This revolt and rebellion by Christians is not simply the rejection of a certain possibility but is also the concomitant struggle for the actualization of an alternative. Here again we see Barth's dialectic at work in negation and affirmation. "In word and deed [Christians] say No here because they may and will say Yes there."[30] This point about revolt and struggle indicates a slight shift in the character of the dialectic. The dialectical situation that gives rise to Christian zeal for the honor of God's name is one of ambiguity and suffering. God is both known and unknown. But Christians pray for the overcoming of this dialectic: they pray that God's name would be glorified, that there would only be light and no darkness. In the struggle for human righteousness the progression towards an eschatological affirmation continues. The No of revolt and rebellion is only possible because of the affirmation of God's Kingdom.

This affirmation makes the revolt of Christians have a special character that distinguishes it from other revolts. The experience of hardship, suffering, and oppression is not what Christians revolt against in their prayer for the coming of the kingdom and their struggle for human righteousness, though the reality of this struggle will mingle with more personal concerns. Christian revolt is not directed against any people, even the most wicked of people. If Christian revolt takes this form, it is only a mistake. "In terms of their commission – even though they will sometimes clash with all kinds of people in discharging it – they rebel and fight for all men, even, and in the last resort precisely, for those with whom they may clash."[31] Christians are for all people because they recognize the common plight that all share, and it is this plight that Christians rebel and revolt against. Struggle *against* this plight is part of how Christians can be *for* all people. They perceive the common solidarity of human beings in this plight, a solidarity that overcomes

---

29 Barth, *The Christian Life*, 288.
30 Barth, *The Christian Life*, 290.
31 Barth, *The Christian Life*, 295.

the other distinctions and conflicts that may emerge from that very plight. Struggle against this plight that is also for all people is constitutive of Christian identity:

> "In all circumstances the Christian is summoned and is in a position to rebel against this plight, to rise up against it, to enter into a conflict with it. This and not men, this plight which is caused by all, for which all are responsible, and which oppresses all, is the enemy between whom and Christians – whose cause is God's and therefore man's – there can and may be no reconciliation or peace. If Christianity were not the *militia Christi*, the *ecclesia militans*, engaged in a struggle with the human plight, it would not be Christianity or the church of Jesus Christ."[32]

At its root, this plight is the disordered form of human life that attempts to be without God and thereby is against God. There is a corresponding rejection of one's fellow human beings that follows from being without and against God. "In offending God they can only offend one another as well."[33] Here again is another layer of dialectic in Barth's ethics. The struggle for human righteous negates, revolts against, and resists the disordered world that is without and against God and other human beings. But this negation depends on the affirmation of all human beings in the cause of God, that they would be with and for God and one another.

Like zeal for the honor of God which depends on the petition that God's name be hallowed, the struggle for human righteousness is first and foremost an invocation of God's action. "The decisive action of [Christian] revolt against disorder, which, correctly understood, includes within itself all others, is their calling upon God in the second petition of the Lord's prayer: 'Thy kingdom come.'"[34] Yet this, what Barth calls the vertical dimension of the struggle, has a concomitant and necessary corresponding horizontal dimension in which Christians seek to establish a human righteousness as (or better, because) they invoke the coming of divine righteousness. And because it is a *human* righteousness, that struggle and whatever steps are taken in that direction will always be infected with the weakness and corruptions of the human will. Yet Christians still can – are required to – seek out human right, freedom, and peace.

---

32   Barth, *The Christian Life*, 296.
33   Barth, *The Christian Life*, 296.
34   Barth, *The Christian Life*, 297.

Negation and Affirmation, Judgment, and Grace

In praying the second petition, Christians are commanded "to live for their part with a view to the coming kingdom."[35] This life has the character of waiting and hastening. Christians await the action of God but do all that they can to run towards it. The character of that running is the struggle for human righteousness. And while human righteousness is not to be confused with the divine righteousness that brings the kingdom, the human righteousness that Christians are to pursue is kingdom-like. It is kingdom-like in its being for human beings and in its resistance against that which threatens human beings. In this context dialectic once again appears, much as it did in the form of Christian witness in the world. Christians must respond with a resolute Yes and No. But when it comes to specific forms and situations, Christians "will think and speak in terms of theses and not principles."[36] The Christian Yes and No in this context can only be partial and not total. "Their total and definitive decision is for man and not for any cause."[37]

A major theme of *The Christian Life* is the marked distinction between what Christians pray for *God* to do, and what Christians can do. This is the difference between God bringing God's kingdom on earth, and the Christian (and all too sinful) struggle for human righteousness that works in anticipation and expectation of that coming kingdom. What links this distinction is the prayer that Christians pray for God's kingdom to come. And what establishes that freedom to pray is that God's kingdom has come, that righteousness has been established in Jesus Christ and his resurrection. This draws a clear line of demarcation between what God will do and has done in bringing the kingdom, and what human beings do in their struggle for righteousness. But it is not just a link. In a very important sense, it is the very distinction between the first and the second, the invocation of the Kingdom and the struggle for human righteousness, that renders the second possible. It would not be possible for Christians to struggle for human righteousness if Christians did not have the freedom to pray that God's kingdom would come. Further, if that coming, and the invocation that God do so, were not distinct from the struggle for human righteousness, then human action which is characterized by the ambiguity of having both knowledge and ignorance of God would be all the more easily and readily confused with divine action.

---

35 Barth, *The Christian Life*, 368.
36 Barth, *The Christian Life*, 375.
37 Barth, *The Christian Life*, 375.

There is an eschatological Yes within which Christian's participate and anticipate during the ambiguous time of suffering the holiness and desecration of God in the world, the simultaneity of righteousness and unrighteousness in the world, the church, and the individual Christian. This Yes is the very basis and hope for the prayer that God's name be hallowed and God's kingdom come. Ultimately, these will happen through God's action. The character of the dialectic seems different here than elsewhere. Barth's dialectic began and focused most strongly on the negation side of the dialectic in *The Epistle to the Romans* whereas here in this last of his theological work, he ends on the side of the eschatological and anticipatory Yes. This final affirmation acknowledges that the dialectical situation is a condition of life between the times, while the hallowing of God's name and the coming of God's Kingdom is awaited. Thus, in the end, the ultimate and final answer, which is thus somehow also the first answer, is God's Yes. Ultimately, the dialectic dissolves into God's affirmation in which all desecration, ignorance, and darkness is abolished by the hallowing of God's name and coming of God's kingdom.

Accountability In General

I define accountability as a relationship status in which the fulfillment of obligations is assessed and sanctioned. Additionally, the purpose of accountability is that the obligations of the relationship would be fulfilled. In an accountability relationship, a judge assesses another's fulfillment of their obligations within their relevant domain(s) according to that domain's norms to apply sanctions based on that assessment. The other party, the accountant, accepts responsibility for fulfilling their obligations such that the judge can assess their fulfillment and apply the appropriate sanctions.[38] When I promise to do

---

38 My account here rests on the pragmatist, Hegelian inferentialism of Robert Brandom, especially as deployed by Jeffrey Stout, John Bowlin and Kevin Hector. See Robert Brandom, *Making It Explicit: Reasoning, Representing, and Discursive Commitment* (Cambridge, MA: Harvard University Press, 1994); *Articulating Reasons: An Introduction to Inferentialism* (Cambridge, MA: Harvard University Press, 2000); *A Spirit of Trust: A Reading of Hegel's Phenomenology* (Cambridge, MA: The Belknap Press of Harvard University Press, 2019); Jeffrey Stout, "Radical Interpretation and Pragmatism: Davidson, Rorty, and Brandom on Truth," in *Radical Interpretation in Religion*, ed. Nancy K. Frankenberry, 1st ed. (Cambridge University Press, 2002); *Democracy and Tradition* (Princeton, NJ: Princeton University Press, 2004); "On Our Interest in Getting Things Right: Pragmatism without Narcissism," in *New Pragmatists*, ed. Cheryl Misak (Oxford: Oxford University Press, 2007), 7–31; John Bowlin, "Barth and Aquinas on Election, Relation-

my breakfast dishes after I get home from work, I am undertaking a commitment and authorizing my wife, Anna to assess and sanction my fulfillment of that obligation. Further, Anna is authorizing me to undertake and fulfill the commitment I have made.

For my purposes here, two components of accountability are most important to highlight: the domain and the obligations. The domain of accountability is simply the area or scope of responsibility within which the obligations of the accountant and (derivatively) the other obligations involved in the accountability relationship hold sway. A real estate agent is only accountable to their clients in the activities they conduct as a real estate agent, and not, for example, as an investment broker or as legal counsel. The real estate agent is also not accountable for their clients qua real estate agent for their clients' parenting or their decisions about where to live and what sort of place to live in.

What partially determines the domain are the obligations taken on by the accountant. Domain is implicitly and explicitly (re)defined in the accountability relationship, and domain can and does change via expansion and contraction, generalization, and specification. An important way in which domain changes is through practices of holding and being held accountable – that is, via the assessment and sanction of the judge. In a promise such as lifelong marriage or similar vows, domain is almost by definition expansive such that the burden is to state what is *excluded* from the responsibilities of the partners to each other, say explicitly via prenuptial agreements. But by default, the domain of responsibility includes far more than the partners can anticipate or plan on – and fidelity despite and through uncertainty is among the assurances that are given when the promises are made. Marriages also frequently involve significant overlap and expansion of domains. The partners are marrying one another, but (in general) they are also incorporating their partner's family and loved ones into their scope of obligation in a way that did not obtain prior.

Obligations partially constitute and determine one another. The promise to do my dishes from breakfast when I get home later occurs in the context of many other salient responsibilities. I am obligated to do the dishes in

---

ship, and Requirement," in *Thomas Aquinas and Karl Barth: An Unofficial Catholic-Protestant Dialogue*, ed. Bruce L. McCormack and Thomas Joseph White (Grand Rapids, MI: Wm. B. Eerdmans Publishing, 2013); *Tolerance among the Virtues* (Princeton, NJ: Princeton University Press, 2016); Kevin Hector, *Theology without Metaphysics: God, Language, and the Spirit of Recognition* (New York: Cambridge University Press, 2011).

my house, regardless of who created the need. I am also obligated to refrain from leaving dishes for someone else to clean, in my case, my wife Anna. That more general obligation is itself governed by our role-responsibilities to one another as spouses who live and work together. Anna and I are also parents to Elias which, among many other obligations, includes the obligation to teach Elias to clean up after himself and for others. I am also obligated (if only to myself) to be present at a certain time and place because of my job. In this instance, I am asserting that I need to delay fulfillment of my dish-doing obligation to avoid reneging my obligation to get to work on time. I am also asserting (here implicitly) that fulfilling my work obligation overrides my dish-doing obligation when they are mutually exclusive.

But my assertion concerning work overriding dishes is also open to examination, challenge, and requests or demands for vindication. At a general level, I would endorse the commitment that my obligations to my family are more important than my professional obligations, and in most cases of competition, I should fulfill my familial obligations and only then my professional ones. So already my claim to being entitled to defer my dish-doing obligation is suspect and in fact would require that my entitlement to that assertion is suspect until I vindicate it. But there is more. In this deferral, I am implying that I would be late or too late to work if I were to rinse my breakfast dishes and put them in the dishwasher. But this hardly requires much time at all, and there are far more likely scenarios that would make me far later than my taking the time to do the dishes would (e.g., forgetting something at home because I am in a hurry, needing to turn back, and then missing the train). Thus, from the path of my general espoused commitments to the specific assertion, my deferral of fulfilling my obligation is not warranted. Anna would thus have every right to challenge that assertion.

Christian Accountability

With this definition of accountability in mind, let's explore what *Christian* accountability involves considering Barth's theology of the Christian life. By "Christian" I have in mind both those who are Christians and Christian commitments more broadly – here through a Barthian lens. My primary claim here is that to be *Christian* is to be *accountable*, and that *Christian* accountability implicates *everyone's* accountability.

Christian accountability is established and constituted by God's own accountability. Through Jesus' atonement, God fulfills God's self-imposed obligation to keep and fully realize the covenant broken by sinful humanity. God assesses and sanctions sinful humanity's failure to meet their obligations in the covenant. Jesus' fulfillment of the covenant reveals and renews God's authority in the world which had broken fellowship with God. God's authority and the kingdom which is so constituted is "shaped and qualified" by God's will and action to say Yes freely and graciously to humanity in Jesus. God's act of might and power in instituting the kingdom, reconciling humanity by judging it is always as the Father and Brother of humanity. God's wrath and judgment is thus not *against* human beings but for them. It *is*, however, against and in conflict with the human being's alienation from God, one's fellows and oneself.[39]

Christians are accountable because constitutive of their identity is their recognition and acknowledgment of their (and everyone's) obligation to God and others: a life of petitioning God for God's aid and action on earth as in heaven. They petition God to do what God has obligated Godself to do: to completely establish God's Kingdom on earth and unambiguously erase everyone's sin that rejects, alienates, and makes an enemy of God and others. Moreover, Christian petition to God also has an obligatory, concomitant action that accords with human capacities in their relationships with themselves, with other Christians, and with the non-Christian world. That is, Christians have accountability relationships in all three of these spheres: they have obligations to God and to the other parties that are assessed and sanctioned. Those obligations take the same form for each: Christians bear witness to Jesus's fulfillment of the broken covenant and revolt against the persistent, pervasive, and pernicious presence of sin prior to God's final establishment of the Kingdom.

Christian recognition and acknowledgment concerns, is on behalf of, and testifies to all humanity. And although fallen humanity does not so recognize and acknowledge God's rule, they are still subject to it:

> "If, however, Christians are to understand themselves as first fruits [...], we cannot avoid the conclusion that in and with what is said primarily and directly to them, to them alone, there is said something prophetically, exemplarily, and

---

[39] "The friendship with which [God] answers man's enmity consists in his making man for his part his friend. He thus reconciles man to himself. The fascinating and mysterious power of the dawning of this hour, the rude incursion of his Kingdom, serves this reconciling. It in this form, manner, and purpose – and no other – that he is Pantokrator, the Almighty" (Barth, *The Christian Life*, 37).

proleptically about the whole race as Christ's people *in spe* (in hope) and therefore about everyone. All men are to be addressed in anticipation precisely in terms of the special responsibility of Christians."[40]

In their accountability to God, Christians recognize and bear witness to the accountability of *everyone* to God through the coming of God's Kingdom.

Christians act in the role of judge in their accountability relationship with the world. They are to assess and sanction the world's fulfillment of *its* obligations just as much as they assess and sanction their own. That assessment takes the general form of the dialectic of affirmation and negation of God and God's reign. In the world, God is both known and unknown, etc. But that dialectic also entails something much finer grained. This is the extremely difficult but extremely important discernment process of assessing the world's and the Christian's fulfillment of their obligations in specific situations, iterations, and instances. In what ways is the world fulfilling its obligations, or not?

The assessment Christians make in these cases determines their own response of sanction to the world, to affirm or deny the actions of the world. But those specific expressions of sanction are nested within a more general form. In ways akin to God's rejection of humanity's rejection of God in sin, Christians are to struggle *against* and *resist* all forms of human rejection of God and the chaos that ensues from it in human life. Conversely, Christians are to struggle *for* all humanity. Like God's Yes, the Christian is called to fight for justice, freedom, and peace in human life against all forms of resistance to it. This means that no particular social form, program, position, or ideology receives the unequivocal Yes or No of Christian witness. Rather, the dialectic of Yes and No constitutes Christian witness in every instance, including the thoughts and actions of Christians in their struggle for human righteousness. Such a dialectical struggle maintains the invocation of Christians for God to do what only God can: to bring forth God's kingdom on earth, to establish God's own holiness and righteousness in the world. The dialectical assessment also acknowledges that such invocation takes the form of an imperfect struggle to establish and maintain an imperfectly human form of righteousness in fulfillment of part of the task of the Christian life.

Zeal for God's honor, the struggle for human righteousness and the dialectic that characterizes them is a form of sanction in Christian accountability. It is a response to the assessment of the human failure to fulfill their cove-

---

40 Barth, *The Christian Life*, 47.

nant obligations, an assessment that only follows from God's fulfilling the covenant on their behalf. The conflict and revolt that is the Christian struggle for human righteousness is an expression of sanction in their accountability relationships. It is a response to the assessment of the sin and disorder of the world, to the unrighteousness that pervades human existence. It is crucial to notice here that the sanction is the Christian taking up common cause with the fallen human being and engage in conflict with the unrighteousness. Christian sanction of human beings per se is solidarity and advocacy. Negative sanction is against those expressions of disorder that desecrate God's name and resist the coming of the kingdom.

That same assessment and sanction from Christians also refracts back upon them, and often in the very forms of unrighteousness they resist. For part of what is required to see the Christian struggle for human righteousness as advocacy of human beings and conflict with sin is the very recognition that is lacking in the world and in the heart of each person – the Christian's heart included. Hence the Christian pursuit of human righteousness is likely to result in their experience of unrighteousness in the rejection or scorn that Jesus suffers. But this is only one part of the story. For such responses presumes that the instance of struggle is legitimate. Yet how many Christian causes, actions and pursuits were conducted under the auspices of a struggle for human righteousness but were not? Such mistaken will and actions is not restricted to ignorance or negligence, nor to malice. In fact, what is more likely according to the dialectics of the Christian life is that such struggles will be taken and treated as efforts that will or are kingdom-like rather than further seeds of corruption. In such cases, sanction is delayed to the future, when Christians suffer under the grace of recognizing the sins of the past for what they and the ways they ripple into the present. But here again, such sanction is also grace and mercy. Yes, it entails and requires suffering, confession, and repentance. But these are gifts in the Christian life. Part of Christian suffering is the recognition of their dire need for God's action, and for the countless way they have sinned against God and their fellows. But that recognition is not case by case alone – there is a sin, and here another – but as a general condition of the Christian life whose manifestations and true nature are unveiled far too late and far too often. Why is this gift and grace, then? Because Christian invocation of God does not begin with sin, nor does it end with it. It begins with the recognition of God's reconciling work in Jesus and endures with the hope that God's kingdom will come, that the promise of the covenant is and will be fulfilled on earth as in heaven.

Fundamental to invocation is the recognition that fulfillment of the covenant in the coming of the Kingdom rests with God alone. And yet their struggle for human righteous echoes the fulfillment of the Kingdom, no matter how faintly or ambiguously. It is the deferral of fulfillment and the recognition that it is not theirs that spurns Christians in their Part of Christian suffering is the recognition of their dire need for God's action, and for the countless way they have sinned against God and their fellows. But that recognition is not case by case alone – there is a sin, and here another – but as a general condition of the Christian life whose manifestations and true nature are unveiled far too late and far too often. Why is this gift and grace, then? Because Christian invocation of God does not begin with sin, nor does it end with it. It begins with the recognition of God's reconciling work in Jesus and endures with the hope that God's kingdom will come, that the promise of the covenant is and will be fulfilled on earth as in heaven. that is the struggle for human righteousness. Similarly, their zeal for God's on is based on their recognition of the certainty of the fulfillment and its present deferral. Rather than cause for passivity, despair, or resignation – even in the struggle – the fulfillment of Christian accountability is a life of hope.[41]

Christians are in accountability relationships. Their accountability relationship with God is the determinative one, but Christians (qua Christians) are in accountability relationships with themselves, other Christians, and the Christian community, and with the world. For Christians to be in accountability relationships, there is a specific task responsibility they have to each of the parties in their accountability relationships. Importantly, the outworking of these relationships, the fulfillment, assessment, and sanction of the obligations of Christians do not necessarily play out separately or in discrete actions. Rather – and this is especially in their accountability relationship with God – these play themselves out simultaneously and often through the same action simply assessed and sanctioned differently depending on the obliga-

---

41 "The tasks of little righteousness which Christians are given when they may pray for the coming of God's kingdom is to see and understand man in his plight from which he cannot rescue himself, but only God can rescue him [...]. Being hopeless, he needs hope. He thus needs – this is the mercy that is to be shown to him – the promise that what he intends and seeks is really there and is there for him. Christians know and have this promise. They know the God who has already created, and in glory will still create, right, worth, freedom, peace, and joy for man. They may hope and live by their hope. To bid man hope, and thus to mediate to him the promise that he needs, is their task" (Barth, *The Christian Life*, 377).

tions and accountability relationships in view. Christians, accountability is a fundamental aspect of what it means to be Christian. Christian participation in the broken covenant fulfilled by Jesus in the atonement also determines their role in their accountability relationships and the meaning of those relationships *per se*.

Accountability In Social, Political Life

In my conception, accountability is a necessary means of establishing and maintaining one's agency, solidarity, and trust with others, and for pursuing human flourishing more generally. Accountability is especially necessary for responding to significant conflicts and harms – especially those that pose a threat to and work to undermine human agency, solidarity, and flourishing. I have argued that Christians ought to acknowledge the ubiquity and persistence of sin in and through their recognition of the reconciling work of God in Christ. That is, there is no proper acknowledgement of sin without first recognizing God's reconciling work, and no striving to remedy sin without presuming and pursuing reconciled relationships with God and others.

In a similar way, the (potentially) deleterious effects of some conflicts and harms occur against the backdrop of striving for and embodying solidarity and flourishing (however poorly or imperfectly) – a backdrop that Christians would proclaim is ultimately rooted in reconciled relationships with God and others. This theological vision redirects the primary focus of such conflicts and harms – what they are ultimately about. They are ultimately (or can be treated as) threats against a reconciled relationship with God and others perpetrated by sin – something that affects and is perpetrated by everyone – via forms of injustice and oppression that do in fact undermine agency, solidarity, and flourishing.

Moreover, the purpose of and ultimate motivation for engaging in these conflicts flows out of and aims for the recognition of and witness to reconciliation with God and others in Christ. The commitment to God's reconciliation in Christ provides the rationale for moving from conditions of injustice to solidarity. The effort to make this shift is – for those who acknowledge it – rooted in God's purpose and rationale for holding humanity accountable: to restore relationship with humanity despite the presence and persistence of sin. Or, in more humanistic terms, the purpose for treating those who have caused harm or perpetrate injustice with dignity and respect is the manifestation of the sort of flourishing, solidarity, and agency that is desired and required from others.

From the perspective of the Christian and of the world, we can see glimpses of worldly or non-Christian accountability. Put differently, we are returning to a general conception of accountability with the insights of Christian accountability now squarely in view.[42] In what follows, I suggest what that accountability might look like and sketch in terms of democratic norms why that conception of accountability might be accepted by those who do not endorse the specifically Christian commitments expressed thus far.

Keeping in some measure of solidarity with those with whom we disagree, have harmed us or even hate us (or whom we hate) is paramount. The impulse to find *some* common ground or common cause with the worst of us – especially in ourselves, and to have compassion for such is not a form of Pollyanna optimism, naive hope, or blissful ignorance of "how things really are." Rather, it is a practice of accountability which maintains solidarity, even at our worst. For those whom we no longer treat as "one of us" or in the space of reasons are no longer accountable or responsible – neither of them to us nor us to them.

In the documentary on Restorative Justice entitled *Circle Up*, Janet Connors, whose son was brutally murdered, makes a powerful statement in this regard:

> "'Who are these monsters?' I remember writing in my journal. I mean, Joel's heart was ripped open […]. They shredded my boy's heart! And then, a couple of days later, I went into my journal and I wrote, 'We're not looking for monsters. We're looking for other young people. We're looking for human beings. If I think of them as monsters, I let them off the hook. 'Cause monsters only do what monsters do. Monsters hurt people. If I hold them in their humanity, then I hold them accountable."[43]

For those whom we cannot or refuse to understand, connect with, and have compassion towards are no longer accountable to us – and we are no longer accountable to them or for them. Think of the horrific conduct and assertions at play in the treatment of indigenous peoples, the environment, those with whom we are at war, the tyrants, the monsters, the demagogues,

---

42 Here I am echoing Kevin Hector's claim that *God's* use of creaturely concepts fulfills and judges *our* use of them. See Hector, *Theology Without Metaphysics*.

43 Janet Connors, *Circle Up*, Documentary, Independently Distributed, 2017, 13:25.

the oppressors. All too often, the first act is to remove "them" from the space of "us." To so demarcate them that they are no longer among us (or never were). For when the separation is complete, "they" are beyond the moral pale. We can do whatever we deem necessary to them for the sake of *us* and those *we* care about. In the vacuum of evacuated accountability, all manner of tyranny, oppression, domination, and horrors take its place.

Nothing I have just said here *requires* adherence to Christian commitments. Rather, I take them to be intrinsically connected to the norms and practices of the democratic tradition articulated by Jeffrey Stout in the immediate aftermath of 9/11 and the "War of Terror." In Stout's words:

> "The solidarity of an aggrieved people can be a dangerous thing. No lesson from recent history could be more evident. Any [people] united mainly by memories of injustices done to it is likely to behave unjustly in its own defense and to elicit similar responses from its neighbors and enemies [...]. Solidarity we will surely need in the struggles ahead. But on what basis shall we secure it? We had better have something in common besides resentful fear [or hatred] of our enemies [...].[44] Part of the democratic program is to involve strangers and enemies, as well as fellow citizens, in the verbal process of holding one another responsible ...] in the hope of drawing undemocratic individuals and groups into the exchange of reasons [...].[45] Strangers and enemies, like the rest of us, employ norms. We therefore press them for reasons and in various other ways hold them accountable for indecencies and cruelties."[46]

We are looking for neither demonization of the other, nor divination of ourselves or our community, but a humble sort of courageous action that speaks boldly and refuses to polarize or sensationalize. Why? Because as tempting as such one-sidedness is; as pervasive and inevitable in public life, in our favored communities, and in our own hearts, these strategies are *not* true forms of accountability. No, they are acts of exoneration in accountability's guise. We must adhere to our common cause in the struggle for human righteousness – whether as Christians bearing witness to the Kingdom of God established by God's reconciliation in Jesus, or as human beings striving to remember and imagine a people who holds to the courage of its highest convictions in the face of the greatest temptations to forsake them.

---

44 Stout, *Democracy and Tradition*, 1.
45 Stout, *Democracy and Tradition*, 13–14.
46 Stout, *Democracy and Tradition*, 197.

Eckhart Chan

The Compromise of Subordination

Tracing the "Positive" Theme in Barth's Church-State Distinction

Introduction

The overarching goal of this paper is not to simply assess the material political implications of Barth's theology, but to bring to the fore the much broader, but still urgent question of how one, in the present time today, should see theology's place in society, and the subsequent demands that has for the way one (re)imagines the theological task and the modes by which they pursue it. The central claim of my proposal is that there are certain "limiting impulses" built into the way Barth coordinates his concept of the Church and the State. I call these "limiting impulses," because I think they are unintentional tendencies implicit within Barth's political thought that actually run counter to the motivating convictions that animate his "theological politics."[1] As a possible remedy for some of these "limiting impulses," I offer Ernst Troeltsch as an unlikely, but nonetheless helpful interlocutor that can serve to both broaden and narrow Barth's political theology in specific key areas. While there are certain historical connections that, I think, make this otherwise unholy union between Barth and Troeltsch rather appropriate on this matter, regardless of the historical plausibility of such a rapprochement of two figures that have come to represent such contrasting theological trajectories, the specific aim of this discussion is to suggest that Troeltsch, when proper-

---

1   In this paper, I will use the terms "theological politics" and "political theology" interchangeably, since Barth would have known of no such distinction within his own thought. Thus, my use of both terms will follow David Haddorff's definition, as that which "speaks about politics within a theological framework and its relationship to the church" (David Haddorff, "Karl Barth's Theological Politics," in *Community State, and Church: Three Essays* [Eugene, OR: Wipf & Stock Publishers, 1960], 3).

ly situated alongside Barth, can help draw out the positive theme in Barth's Church-State distinction.

Section 1 – Tensions within Barth's Church-State Distinction

In this first section, I begin by turning to the shape of Barth's account of the Church-State relation, especially as he develops it in his 1946 essay, "The Christian Community and the Civil Community." While one could locate a number of other entry points into the various ways Barth parses the Church-State relation throughout his life and oeuvre, not to mention the two other texts of this colloquium, Barth's 1935 address "Gospel and Law" and his 1938 "Church and State," I have chosen to focus on the 1946 essay because of the pivotal shift that occurs here. This shift is given in the title of the essay, which is that Barth translates the Church-State relation to that between the Christian *community* and the civil *community*. Here, from the outset, Barth explains that the purpose of reformulating the Church-State relation in terms of "community" is that it helps to highlight not only the "positive relationship and connexion between them," but it also serves as a reminder that when one speaks of the "Church" and the "State," they are speaking "not merely and primarily with institutions and offices but with human beings gathered together in corporate bodies in the service of common tasks."[2] While the Church and the State may not be wholly reducible to the individuals which they are constituted by, neither can they ever be understood in separation from the communities which they are constituted for.

If one looks just at the trajectory of Barth's account of the Church-State relation throughout the three essays from 1935 to 1946, this is a pivotal turn in Barth's conceptualization of the theological political question. This move establishes, for Barth, a positive theological understanding of the State, while also securing the dialectical hinge by which the Church-State relation is maintained. By drawing both Church and State into relation with one another under the prism of human community, the Church too now comes to stand firmly under God's "No," while subsequently the world comes to stand alongside the Church within God's "Yes." In other words, the Church-

---

2   Karl Barth, "The Christian Community and the Civil Community," in *Community State, and Church: Three Essays* (Eugene, OR: Wipf & Stock Publishers, 1960), 149.

State distinction becomes subsumed and understood within the broader framework of Barth's God-World relation.[3]

This stands as one of the strongest aspects of Barth's dynamic and decidedly eschatological intervention into the question of political theology,[4] for in situating the Church and State together as concentric circles ordered to the coming Kingdom of God, Barth relativizes the entire Church-State relation not simply by an act of negation but by folding the one into the other within a positive dialectical relation. Therefore, although of course, for Barth, the Church occupies the "inner circle" and the State the "outer circle," this is no claim for the Church's superiority over the State, rather, the opposite. As Barth says, "The Christian community is aware of the need for the civil community, and it alone takes the need absolutely seriously."[5] The crucial point here is that the thrust of Barth's relativizing move is not to threaten the legitimacy of either institution, but rather to soften the misleading distinction between the two that gives the impression that the Church and the State exist as separate, self-contained, self-sufficient authorities that must inevitably exist in competitive tension.

In this way, by locating the Church as the inner circle of the State, the Church – or better yet, the Christian community – comes to be understood as existing for the sake of the outer circle, which is not only "the State," but the whole community of humanity in all states. To quote Barth, "Since the Church is ecumenical (catholic) by virtue of its very origin, [...] It will always seek to serve the best interests of the particular city or place where it is stationed. But it will never do this without at the same time looking out beyond the city walls."[6] Thus, this forms a dynamic relation in which the Church and State as two concentric circles are not enclosed with bold, impermeable lines, but must be seen as being bordered by something like a perforated edge.[7]

This positive dialectical relation supplies the subversive force of Barth's famous "witness" concept. The Church does not stand above the State, ruling it by force of divine mandate. Instead, this inner circle must be understood as existing, in some sense, within and below the State. For the Church serves

---

3   J. N. J Kritzinger, "'The Christian in Society': Reading Barth's Tambach Lecture (1919) in its German Context," *HTS Theological Studies* 63, no. 4 (May 2007): 1674.
4   Joshua Mauldin, *Barth, Bonhoeffer, & Modern Politics* (Oxford: Oxford University Press, 2021), 48–49.
5   Barth, "The Christian Community and the Civil Community," 154–155.
6   Barth, "The Christian Community and the Civil Community," 178.
7   Barth, "The Christian Community and the Civil Community," 158–159.

the State not as a sanctifying institution that crowns the civil authorities with a veneer of divine might, but as that disenchanting community which works to safeguard against all attempts to divinize the political.[8] Barth explains,

> "The *polis* has walls. Up till now, at least, civil communities have always been more or less clearly marked off from one another [...]. And that is why the State has no safeguard or corrective against the danger of either neglecting or absolutizing itself and its particular system [...]."[9]

Put simply, according to Barth, the civil community needs the Christian community, because the Christian community acts to relativize and break down the artificial and pernicious walls, so often built up by state industrial complexes, that threaten the livelihood of the actual civil community itself.[10]

However, here, one must not fail to see the full force of Barth's eschatological reformulation of the Church-State distinction. For while this does clear ample ground on which Barth can launch a thoroughly theological critique of the State, the relativizing eschatological horizon of the Kingdom of God is a double-edged sword that also exacts a critique of the Church, one that perhaps is even more devastating than that addressed to the State.[11] The crucial word for the Church is that its subversive role within the State does not derive from any source of authority from within itself, but only from its witnessing of the revelation of the coming Kingdom, such that "even at its best the Church is not an image of the Kingdom of God."[12] What this means is that the Church relativizes the State not because it embodies some timeless, eternal Absolute, but because the Church is that body which recognizes its

---

8   Christophe Chalamet, "Karl Barth and the Weimar Republic," in *The Weimar Moment: Liberalism, Political Theology, and Law*, ed. Leonard V. Kaplan and Rudy Koshar (Lanham, MD: Lexington Books, 2012), 250.
9   Barth, "The Christian Community and the Civil Community," 151–152.
10 George Hunsinger, "Toward a Radical Barth," in *Karl Barth and Radical Politics*, ed. and trans. George Hunsinger (Philadelphia, PA: Westminster Press, 1976), 186.
11 As Robert Jenson perceptively notes: "The *Commentary on Romans* is ambiguous. It is the document of the end of Christian religion; it poses to us the question: faith in a future or the religious quest for assuagement of time? If we pose this question *back to it*, we immediately see that it can be interpreted either way. The book is an attack on Christian religion, but could as well be read as an apology for an unhistorical, unchristian religion as for an anti-religious Christianity" (Robert Jenson, *God After God: The God of the Past and the God of the Future, As Seen in the Work of Karl Barth* [Minneapolis, MN: Fortress Press, 2010], 52).
12 Barth, "The Christian Community and the Civil Community," 168.

own relativism and in doing so does not seek to absolutize itself.[13] As Barth's famous maxim goes, "Men are men, and God is God."[14] What Barth so promisingly sketches out here is a thoroughly theological account of a politics of humility, wherein the Church can only proceed by total dependence on the movement of the Holy Spirit.[15] This does not amount to some privileged ethical viewpoint, but only in a cautious confidence that knows well that all our ethical judgments exist within a greater judgment.[16] Here, Barth reminds the reader of "the fifth thesis of the *Theological Declaration of Barmen* (1934), [that] the Christian community also exists in 'the still unredeemed world,' [...] The Word and Spirit of God are no more automatically available in the Church than they are in the State."[17]

The theme I have traced here is Barth's attempt to take the world seriously, in its entirety – both Church, State, and all other communities in-between – as God's world.[18] Seen from this angle, the central motivating question of Barth's overarching political theology is not simply with demarcating the limits of the State, but with how the Church ought to serve the State. For even in the Church's critique of the State, this is a critique that does not end with its "No," but always rests in a prior and deeper "Yes," because the Church exists "unconditionally for all men, for the common cause of the whole State."[19]

Naturally, Barth's politics would appear under the banner of various articulations between his early years in Safenwil and his eventual return to Switzerland. Nevertheless, the salient point here is that this positive theme is already present in Barth's early political theology. From his two lectures in 1911, "Jesus Christ and the Movement for Social Justice" and "Human Right and Civic Duty," on through both editions of the Romans commentary, as well as his Münster and Bonn lectures on ethics,[20] this thread is, I think, the boldest and most promising aspect of Barth's political thought, for what

---

13 Mauldin, *Barth, Bonhoeffer, and Modern Politics*, 39.
14 Karl Barth, *The Epistle to the* Romans, trans. Sir Edwyn Clement Hoskyns (Oxford: Oxford University Press, 1968), 63.
15 Karl Barth, *Ethics*, ed. Dietrich Braun, trans. Geoffrey W. Bromiley (Edinburgh: T&T Clark, 1981), 399–451.
16 Haddorff, "Karl Barth's Theological Politics," 45.
17 Barth, "The Christian Community and the Civil Community," 152.
18 Wolfhart Pannenberg, "The Basis of Ethics in the Thought of Ernst Troeltsch," in *Ethics*, trans. Keith Crim (Philadelphia, PA: Westminster Press; London: Search Press, 1981), 110.
19 Barth, "The Christian Community and the Civil Community," 183.
20 Chalamet, "Karl Barth and the Weimar Republic," 243–244, 250–252.

Barth attempts to do by taking the eschatological kingdom of God as the beginning and end point of all theology,[21] is to secure a Christian political ethic that is wholly free to live in and for the World as a witness to the divine goodness of all humanity.[22] To be clear, this is not some amorphous freedom to will the good of all people in a hopelessly general and abstract dimension, rather, it is the concrete freedom for the Christian community to abandon itself, without fear, for "the lower and lowest levels of human society. The poor, the socially and economically weak and threatened."[23] In this way, the Christian community is enabled to confidently, yet cautiously enter into the complexities that come with the encounter of actual, particular human persons. What this implies is that within Barth's either-or between the Kingdom of God and the World, there exists something like a both-and between the Church and the State.

However, the obvious issue here is that the view I have provided of this positive theme in Barth's Church-State distinction is not the way in which Barth's political theology, even in its mature form, has always been received.[24] Especially when compared to Harnack's judgment of Barth's project as a form of "sectarian apocalypticism,"[25] or Niebuhr's quip that "if the Barthians are socialists, I think it is not unfair to them to say that they don't work very hard at it,"[26] or perhaps most provocatively, the claim advanced by Falk Wag-

---

21 Bruce L. McCormack, *Karl Barth's Critically Realistic Dialectical Theology: Its Genesis and Development 1909–1936* (Oxford: Clarendon Press, 1997), 32.
22 Chalamet, "Karl Barth and the Weimar Republic," 256–257.
23 Barth, "The Christian Community and the Civil Community," 173.
24 Jeffrey Stout, following Hunsinger's reading of Barth's political theology, is an exemplary exception. See Jeffrey Stout, *Democracy and Tradition* (Princeton, NJ: Princeton University Press, 2004), 108–111.
25 Gary Dorrien, "Barthian Dialectics 'Yes' and 'No' on the Barthian Revolt and its Legacy," in *The Weimar Moment: Liberalism, Political Theology, and Law*, ed. Leonard V. Kaplan and Rudy Koshar (Lanham, MD: Lexington Books, 2012), 223.
26 Reinhold Niebuhr, *Essays in Applied Christianity*, ed. D.B. Robertson (New York: Meridian Books, 1959), 148. In many respects, my critique of Barth in this paper is a fine-tuning of Niebuhr's: "Karl Barth on the other hand deals realistically with the existential factors revealed in the justice of an actual community in his *Christengemeinde und Buergergemeinde*. But he is rather unnecessarily cryptic and embarrassed about the fact that there are implied standards of 'natural law' in his discussion of the justice of a state. He declares that he is not ashamed of possible affinities between his thought and 'natural law' concepts but declines to elucidate the point further. Ultimately he comes to some rather curious conclusions about the source of justice in the civil society. 'The divine ordinance of the state,' he declares, 'makes it quite possible that it may in its own sphere come to quite

ner and the "Munich school," but even suggested by Pannenberg,[27] that there exists in Barth's theology a "fascist structure,"[28] the picture on display here of Barth's positive political theology appears rather unrecognizable. But this is not to say that these critics of Barth are necessarily wrong. In fact, quite to the contrary, there are, I think, good reasons why Barth has so often been taken up in this negative way by his critics.

Section 2 – Subordination as Compromise

The relevant question of this second section is not with who reads Barth correctly, but with how one can parse Barth's underlying theological-political intentions from within the internal, sometimes contradictory, tensions of Barth's dialectical patterns of thought – or what I earlier referred to as the "limiting impulses" within Barth's political theology. My suggestion is that the strength of Barth's relativizing approach to the political question is simultaneously its limitation.[29] For Barth, in attempting to safeguard against all claims of absoluteness through an unrelenting insistence on the exclusively eschatological nature of the Kingdom of God,[30] does so at the expense of backing himself deeper into a treacherous dualism he inherits from Herrmann's neo-Kantianism.[31] This dualism is that between faith and knowledge, revelation and history, the Kingdom of God and the world, or as Wilfried

---

correct theoretic and practical decisions, even though one might, considering the dubious source of the judgment, expect nothing but error and misadventure.' This means that the standards of justice in any society are so corrupted by sin that only a mysterious overruling providence achieves the kind of social harmony and peace which we know in some states. Actually the justice of the most healthy human communities is not as mysterious as that. It is a revelation of man's residual capacity for justice, despite the corruptions of self-interest in his standards and in his practices" (Reinhold Niebuhr, *Faith and History: A Comparison of Christian and Modern Views of History* [London: Nisbet & Co., 1949], 221).

27 Wolfhart Pannenberg, *Systematic Theology*, Vol. 2, trans. Geoffrey W. Bromiley (Edinburgh: T&T Clark, 1994), 431–432.
28 Eberhard Jüngel, *Karl Barth: A Theological Legacy*, trans. Garrett E. Paul (Philadelphia, PA: Westminster Press, 1986), 14.
29 Dorrien, "Barthian Dialectics 'Yes' and 'No' on the Barthian Revolt and its Legacy," 209.
30 Jüngel, *Karl Barth*, 103.
31 Bruce L. McCormack, "Revelation and History in Transfoundationalist Perspective: Karl Barth's Theological Epistemology in Conversation with a Schleiermachian Tradition," in *Orthodox and Modern: Studies in the Theology of Karl Barth* (Grand Rapids, MI: Baker Academic, 2008), 28–30.

Groll polemically puts it, the "absolute distinction between Christianity and the non-Christian world."[32]

Of course, this is not a new criticism of the "consistent eschatology" that is so characteristic of Barth's early theology, one that even Barth would later go on to make of his second *Romans* commentary.[33] However, the crucial contention here, following Christoph Gestrich's pneumatological revision of Barth, is that even after his final Christological shift in the *Church Dogmatics* there seems to remain a lingering disjunction between two theological trajectories within the theme of Christ's universal rule.[34] Barth gives the reader a glimpse of this problematic tension in his lectures on the Apostles' Creed, delivered only several years prior to the 1946 essay at the focus of our present discussion: "Every man is under the dominion of Christ, whether he knows it or does not know it. [...] The difference between the Church and the world is that in the Church the Lord of the world is acknowledged and confessed, whereas in the world he is still ignored. But the same Lord rules over both."[35] The subtle difficulty Barth runs up against in trying to situate the Church and the world alongside each other is that on the one hand, there is the priority of the Word of God and the attending primacy of the Church, which, while not above the civil community, nevertheless stands as its inner circle. Yet, on the other hand, there is the Church, the Christian community, that stands together with the civil community before the gracious judgment of the Word of God, which is no less available in the world as it is in the Church.[36] The common critique here is that Barth in the end is not dialectical enough, and because of this his ethics are left immobile.[37] To quote Pannenberg, it is the "exclusive nature of [Barth's] theology of revelation that thwarted [his] intention to think the world without any qualifications as God's world, and that

---

32 Wilfried Groll, *Ernst Troeltsch und Karl Barth: Kontinuität im Widerspruch*, Beiträge zur evangelischen Theologie, 72 (Munich: Kaiser, 1976), 106ff, quoted in Pannenberg, "The Basis of Ethics in the Thought of Ernst Troeltsch," 110.
33 McCormack, *Karl Barth's Critically Realistic Dialectical Theology*, 288–290.
34 John Macken, *The Autonomy Theme in the Church Dogmatics: Karl Barth and His Critics* (Cambridge: Cambridge University Press, 1990), 140.
35 Karl Barth, *The Faith of the Church: A Commentary on the Apostles' Creed According to Calvin's Catechism*, trans. Gabriel Vahanian (Eugene, OR: Wipf & Stock Publishers, 2006), 111.
36 Macken, *The Autonomy Theme in the Church Dogmatics*, 139–141.
37 Dorrien, "Barthian Dialectics 'Yes' and 'No' on the Barthian Revolt and its Legacy," 212.

led instead to a self-imposed isolation of Christian faith and thought in an imaginary realm apart from the real human world."[38]

An anecdote from later in Barth's theological career that helps to illustrate this tension well is Barth's response to the organizing theme of the 1948 Assembly of the World Council of Churches. The theme was titled, "The Disorder of the World and God's Design." Barth, in predictable fashion, took issue with the fundamental premise of the theme. For Barth, the organizers of the WCC had gotten the question backwards; it was not the Church's job to try to fix the world. To be sure, this was not because Barth was committed to a holy indifference towards the world, but because he believed all Christian talk about the world must always begin with the already victorious Word of God.[39] As one might expect, this was not the most popular stance to take, especially at the very first Assembly of the WCC. Barth had hoped that perhaps at least Niebuhr would stand by his side, but in the end, Barth, as he had done so often throughout his life, stood alone in his conviction.[40]

There is, I think, much to admire about Barth in this regard, and of course, the general critique that has been outlined is not new and could be rebuffed in a number of ways.[41] However, the relevant issue here is the tension within Barth's theological politics that is illustrated by the exchange in 1948. My specific concern is that against Barth's best intentions to articulate a Christian political ethic marked by the freedom and power of God's definitive word of affirmation, too often, Barth's fierce insistence on Jesus himself being the *kerygma* of the already-victorious, coming Kingdom did not leave much space for anything else to be said.[42] In more specific terms, despite Barth's attempt to enliven constructive Christian political action, because of the lingering dualism implicit within his "eschatological reservation,"[43] which he employs to think the Church alongside the State and vice versa,

---

38 Pannenberg, "The Basis of Ethics in the Thought of Ernst Troeltsch," 110.
39 Stanley Hauerwas, "Barth and Reinhold Niebuhr," in *The Wiley Blackwell Companion to Karl Barth, Volume 2: Barth in Dialogue*, ed. George Hunsinger and Keith L. Johnson (Chichester, West Sussex: John Wiley & Sons, 2020), 637.
40 Dorrien, "Barthian Dialectics 'Yes' and 'No' on the Barthian Revolt and its Legacy," 233.
41 See Christopher Asprey, *Eschatological Presence in Karl Barth's Göttingen Theology* (Oxford: Oxford University Press, 2010), 11–16.
42 Bruce McCormack, "The Spirit of the Lord is Upon Me: Pneumatological Christology with and beyond Barth," in *The Spirit is Moving: New Pathways in Pneumatology*, ed. Gijsbert van den Brink, Eveline van Staalduine-Sulman, and Maarten Wisse (Leiden; Boston: Brill, 2019) 133–134.
43 McCormack, "Revelation and History in Transfoundationalist Perspective," 32.

Barth incidentally cordons Christianity off to an inexpressible and immaterial eschatological realm.[44] Robert Jenson puts this well in his reading of Barth's *Romans*,

> "Thus the gospel is a proclamation of a future hope *with a narrative* content. But in the *Commentary on Romans* it has become an eternal event, of which nothing can be narrated. [...] A consistent policy based on the *Commentary on Romans* would be a portentous silence, which might be religiously impressive, but would mark the cessation of the gospel."[45]

Certainly, as already mentioned, Barth attempted to move beyond this difficulty in his later years, nevertheless, the precise point of my contention is that the 1948 incident at the WCC evinces a proclivity towards political quietism, or even a sectarian *temptation*, which remained throughout Barth's life and work.[46]

The challenge this presents for Barth's political thought is that it imbeds within his account of the Church's witness a tendency to drift into an indirect, passive subordination to the State, whereby the Church's prophetic speech is turned in on itself, consumed by the preoccupation with properly maintaining the eschatological reservation of its proclamation. The irony here is that in this posture, when the Church is confronted by its own context – with concrete politics, policies, and persons – it often struggles to find anything politically meaningful to say, because it is so busy policing the speech of its own community. This tension within Barth's theological political thought is where, as Eberhard Jüngel explains, "the political is surely a predicate of theology, but theology is never a predicate of the political."[47] This runs under Barth's strong (and commendable) insistence that God is a talkative God on the one hand, but on the other hand, Barth's frequent conflation of the need to limit the epistemological hubris of human God-talk with that of limiting the voices of others. To put it simply, for Barth, God speaks, but at times, it oddly feels like a rather one-sided conversation.

---

44 In response to Asprey, while I am building upon the common critiques of Barth made by the likes of Jenson, Pannenberg, and Gunton, I am not claiming this dualism is integral to Barth's system. Rather, I am only suggesting that this dualistic tendency nonetheless remains as an impulse within the dynamics of his political thought.
45 Jenson, *God after God*, 31.
46 It is no coincidence that Yoder and Hauerwas have found rich resources in Barth for their respective postliberal programs.
47 Jüngel, *Karl Barth*, 104.

Admittedly, caution does need to be heeded here, for the "critique" of Barth that I am proposing is not really meant to be a critique in the full sense of the term. Instead, the purpose of drawing out this criticism is to show how the positive and the negative, the active and the passive exist as two dialectical, but sometimes competing tensions and trajectories within Barth's theological politics. This could help explain, at least in part, what has appeared at times in Barth's material politics to be a certain degree of inconsistency or even indecisiveness.[48]

To further sharpen the point, it is crucial to see that the exact location of the problem does not lie with Barth's radical eschatology, but rather the crux of the problem lies with Barth's continued assumption, albeit implicitly, of the dualism alluded to at the beginning of this section between revelation and history. What can be discerned at the limit of Barth's political theology is that at the heart of this dualism is a fraught distinction, originating from the mediating theologies of Ritschl and Herrmann, between theology and religion, or what Troeltsch calls the "agnostic theory" of religious knowledge.[49] As is well known, the question of theological epistemology was at the heart of the pivotal debates over the essence of Christianity that dominated the nineteenth century,[50] and during the course of these debates, Herrmann and Troeltsch came to represent two major competing alternatives towards the task of thinking Christianity's identity. From Troeltsch's end, the debate revolved around the hopeless dualism of Herrmann's theological epistemology, from which he "utterly banished every kind of philosophy of religion, and using experience of Jesus as his criterion set Christianity as the only religion over against everything non-Christian as being non-religion."[51] The point here is that although Barth would eventually break from Herrmann in search of a new "critically realistic" starting point,[52] Barth remained tied to the debate between Herrmann and Troeltsch in so far as he himself would come to offer his own unique answer to the essence question, but with that also

---

48 For example, the divergence in Barth's response to National Socialism versus Soviet Communism. Dorrien, "Barthian Dialectics 'Yes' and 'No' on the Barthian Revolt and its Legacy," 210.
49 Ernst Troeltsch, "Half a Century of Theology: A Review," in *Writings on Theology and Religion*, ed. and trans. Robert Morgan, Michael Pye (Louisville, KY: John Knox Press, 1977), 58–59.
50 Stephen Sykes, *The Identity of Christianity: Theologians and the Essence of Christianity from Schleiermacher to Barth* (London: SPCK, 1984), 193.
51 Troeltsch, "Half a Century of Theology: A Review," 74–75.
52 McCormack, *Karl Barth's Critically Realistic Dialectical Theology*, 67–68.

persisted a lingering dualism between Christianity and the non-Christian world.[53]

This historical connection is significant, and while it deserves more careful treatment than this paper can supply, for our present purposes it helps bring into focus another decidedly theological political trajectory – emerging from the impending crisis of a century tottering on collapse – that also takes as its political horizon the absolute eschatological nature of the Kingdom of God, but now without the impediment of Herrmann's dualism; this is the path taken up by Ernst Troeltsch.[54] It is rarely acknowledged, but it is no coincidence that Barth and Troeltsch both share this core eschatological thread in their political thought. The reason for this is because Barth's refashioning of theology on the grounds of God's sovereign action in the Word of God was, effectively, a radicalization of Troeltsch's eschatological reframing of the debates surrounding the identity of Christianity, wherein, for Troeltsch, Christianity remains beyond any single, static, externally identifiable essence.[55] According to Troeltsch's interpretation of the failed parousia, it is precisely the unfulfilled eschatological reality of the Kingdom that paradoxically creates the condition of possibility for the world to be taken seriously as constitutive of the continual task of Christianity's (re)articulation.[56]

---

53 McCormack, "Revelation and History in Transfoundationalist Perspective," 39.
54 Of particular note is Barth's striking invocation of Troeltsch towards the end of his 1919 Tambach lecture: "It is only in *God* that the synthesis can be found; but in God it *can* be found – the synthesis which is *meant* in the thesis and *sought* in the antithesis. Troeltsch has the striking sentence in his *Social Doctrines* (Soziallehren), 'The energy of the life here is the energy of the life beyond,' and we add: this is the energy of affirmation and the greater energy of denial" (Karl Barth, "The Christian's Place in Society," in *The Word of God and The Word of Man*, trans. Douglas Horton [New York: Harper & Row, 1957], 322). Christophe Chalamet has pointed out that this was a popular quote from Troeltsch, taken from the closing paragraph of the *Soziallehren*, that Barth repeatedly referred to throughout both his early and later writings. And while we should be careful not to assign too much weight to a single quotation, the themes in "The Christian's Place in Society" of the disjunction between the Kingdom of God and the world, of the fundamental contingency of all human life, of the constructive, God-given unrest of the present, and of the synthesis which can only be found in God, give reason to read in this lecture an indirect critique of Troeltsch. Christophe Chalamet, "Redemption of This World—Reflections on Eschatology in Light of Barth's Dogmatic Lectures in Münster (1925–1926)," in *The Finality of the Gospel: Karl Barth and the Tasks of Eschatology*, Studies in Reformed Theology, 43 (Leiden, The Netherlands: Brill, 2022), 147.
55 Sykes, *The Identity of Christianity*, 193.
56 Pannenberg, "The Basis of Ethics in the Thought of Ernst Troeltsch," 105–107.

While this dynamic does bear a similarity to the positive theme seen with Barth in the first section of this paper, Barth makes the decisive move beyond Troeltsch's "historicist eschatology" by tying it to the unchanging Word of God.[57] In this way, Barth represents, what Stephen Sykes has called, "the apotheosis of the inwardness tradition,"[58] since Barth takes Troeltsch's bold deabsolutizing of all essence talk regarding Christianity's identity and pushes it beyond even its furthest end, past the outer limit of all subjectivity until he arrives upon the new ground of the "objectively real 'self-presupposing divine subjectivity.'"[59] The critique I have been carefully trying to pinpoint in this section finds its culmination here, for it is this move that ultimately confines Barth to an eschatological reservation, which, although intended to attest to the free and undomesticated nature of the Word of God, incidentally re-establishes a dualism that locks up Barth's political theology from fully engaging the world.[60]

However, this is not the necessary political endpoint of Barth's eschatological trajectory. In fact, while there is much more that can be said about Barth's connection to Troeltsch, the upshot of this juxtaposition is to show that the dualistic impasse Barth runs up against may be a tendency inherent within his political theology, but by no means is it an inevitable outcome. This is where Troeltsch proves helpful. For Troeltsch, rather than arriving at a concept of "witness" or "subordination," the eschatological horizon frees the Church to seek temporary "compromises" or provisional "syntheses" with the World. Undoubtedly, terms like "compromise" and "synthesis" will worry any faithful reader of Barth.[61] Nevertheless, although space does not permit for a comprehensive analysis of these two concepts that span Troeltsch's ethical, socio-political, historical, and theological thought, close attention to the animating concerns and practical applications of Troeltsch's conception of compromise and synthesis draw him noticeably closer to Barth's positive

---

57 Judith Wolfe, "The Eschatological Turn in German Philosophy," *Modern Theology* 35, no. 1 (January 2019): 58–60.
58 Sykes, *The Identity of Christianity*, 192–193.
59 McCormack, *Karl Barth's Critically Realistic Dialectical Theology*, 67.
60 Sykes, *The Identity of Christianity*, 193–196.
61 "Obviously the concept of synthesis would be the least Christian of all, for it would mean no more and no less than trying to achieve God's miraculous act ourselves. In faith and in the thinking of faith there can be no thought of synthesis. Faith means recognizing that synthesis cannot be attained and committing it to God and seeking and finding it in Him" (Karl Barth, *Church Dogmatics*, I/1, 2nd ed., ed. G. W. Bromiley and T. F. Torrance, trans. G. W. Bromiley [New York: T&T Clark, 2005], 175).

definition of the Church's subordination, wherein "the subordination accrues to the good of the civil community however well or however badly that community is defended, because the civil cause (and not merely the Christian cause) is also the cause of the one God."[62]

Of crucial note here is that for both Barth and Troeltsch, Christianity relates to the political order only indirectly because of the eschatological nature of the message of the gospel. As Troeltsch says, echoing Barth's articulation of the disenchanting function of the Church, "Christianity does away with the self-sufficiency of the state by subordinating the state to the kingdom of God."[63] Clearly, for Barth, the gospel's indirect relation to the political realm is itself political. In no way is it meant to be an injunction against political engagement, but quite the contrary, it is the condition of possibility for political action. In a similar vein, Troeltsch often speaks of Christianity having no inherent politics, yet, just as with Barth, for Troeltsch this in no way means the abdication of responsibility among Christians in the political arena. Instead, this is what provides the impetus for Troeltsch's account of Christianity's constructive political task, a task which is necessarily characterized by the continual formation of provisional compromises and syntheses. To quote Troeltsch once more, and now we can begin to hear more clearly the positive theme consonant with Barth's distinctively *theological* politics, "What we are concerned with, therefore, is not so much a Christian political ethic as the contribution of the Christian ethic to political ethics."[64] Unquestionably, there is a theological gulf that stands between Barth and Troeltsch, yet even so, the key takeaway here is not that Troeltsch, in contrast to Barth, as suggested in the introduction to our text, "uncritically view[s] the state as the redemptive or the 'divine state'...[creating] a *synthesis* between church and state."[65] While this is how Troeltsch is often portrayed, it stands far removed from the actual critical aim of Troeltsch's sophisticated concept of "synthesis."[66] This is not a simple, one-sided political theology of cultural accommodation; this is, at least in intent, a thoroughly theological politics, much like Barth's, in so far as it is an attempt to – following David Haddorff's definition

---

62 Barth, "The Christian Community and the Civil Community," 159–160.
63 Ernst Troeltsch, "Political Ethics and Christianity," in *Religion in History*, trans. James Luther Adams and Walter F. Bense (Minneapolis, MN: Fortress Press, 1991), 203.
64 Troeltsch, "Political Ethics and Christianity," 202.
65 Haddorff, "Karl Barth's Theological Politics," 54.
66 Mark Chapman, *Ernst Troeltsch and Liberal Theology* (Oxford: Oxford University Press, 2001), 8.

– "speak about politics within a theological framework and its relationship to the church."⁶⁷

The payoff of this connection lies in the subtle, but crucial difference between Barth and Troeltsch within this context, which is that Troeltsch places the emphasis in his articulation of the Church-State distinction on the open-ended, ever-evolving, mutually informing relation as central to the Church's political task. Precisely because Christianity has no intrinsic political theory it must necessarily strive to work alongside other interlocuters in approaching the political question as it awaits the yet-to-be-realized eschatological Kingdom of God. In contrast, Barth's articulation of the Church-State distinction tends to be more restrained on the prospect of fruitful cooperation between the Church and the State given his methodological commitment to the priority of the Word of God.

Section 3 – The Figure of the Theologian

The following bears mentioning: a major reason why Troeltsch has a more straightforward path towards affirming a positive political theology is because his eschatological reservation is not saddled, at least not to the same extent as Barth, by the Herrmannian dualism between revelation and history. Of course, this is partly due to the fact that Troeltsch has a relatively bare Christology, especially when compared to Barth, the alleged "christomonist." For many, this is enough to turn away from Troeltsch, but oftentimes in their haste, what is overlooked is that Troeltsch's theological project approximates in interesting ways the kind of pneumatocentric trajectory characteristic of Barth's early years in Göttingen. Although far beyond the scope of this study of Barth, suffice it to say that at times Troeltsch does appear to allude to an underlying notion of revelation that coordinates both the Church and the world as coequal sites of the Spirit's inbreaking, such that the truth of Christianity is not in any way confined to the Church, but always potentially available outside of it as well.

Nevertheless, the important distinction that must be made here is the question of public theology from the question of theological epistemology.⁶⁸ When it comes to the latter, due to the priority Barth assigns to the Word of God, the dualism implicit in his political theology is ultimately unavoidable

---

67 Haddorff, "Karl Barth's Theological Politics," 3.
68 Macken, *The Autonomy Theme in the Church Dogmatics*, 140.

The Compromise of Subordination

as an inherent *tendency*. Thus, if one were to think with Barth, they must reckon with the implications of his Christology, which does theoretically allow for the occasional possibility of revelation in the world, apart from the Church, yet, it is a possibility that must always remain only an open question.[69] Obviously from this standpoint, Barth stands worlds apart from Troeltsch. However, when it comes to the question of theology's service to the world, an illuminating convergence appears in the kind of political posture that both Troeltsch and Barth call for in their respective political theologies. For example, especially noteworthy is Troeltsch's remarkable final paragraph of his essay, "On the Possibility of a Liberal Christianity":

> "We may look upon the task we are setting for ourselves as intrinsically possible, even though we must not underestimate the enormous difficulties. [...] The theologians, professional philosophers, and religionists, who are generally charged with these matters [...] are not by themselves able to provide these. They can do no more than to keep the spark glowing, to prepare for the future, and to break their bread for as many as come seeking it. Those who become anxious and dejected under these circumstances must cling to the inner assurance that is the foundation of all religion, that God is the Lord of the world and of history, that even the present changes and situations are created and fulfilled by God, and that we, with the movement of our own life, stand in the movement of God's life. Whatever may become of our search for a liberal Christianity, God sits on the Divine throne (*im Regiment*) with God's truth prevailing. What counts is not that we save Christianity but that we trust in the victory of God. What we perceive to be the truth binding our conscience cannot be wholly false and must point toward the future. We may devote ourselves, therefore, seriously and faithfully to the task that we comprehend, and leave the rest to God. For the present is no more without God than any other time ever was."[70]

The proposal I would like to offer is that in this specific context, Troeltsch and Barth need not necessarily be read in total opposition to one another. This is not to claim that there can be some sort of dogmatic reconciliation between the two. Instead, the relevant aim here is to highlight how Troeltsch can help safeguard against sectarian impulses within Barth's theological politics. By bringing Barth's concept of subordination into closer proximity with Troeltsch's concept of compromise, new pathways for deepening and furthering the positive theme in Barth's Church-State distinction can be

---

69 Macken, *The Autonomy Theme in the Church Dogmatics*, 140–141.
70 Ernst Troeltsch, "On the Possibility of a Liberal Christianity (1910)," in *Religion in History*, trans. James Luther Adams and Walter F. Bense (Minneapolis, MN: Fortress Press, 1991), 359.

unveiled. In this way, Troeltsch, I think, helps to draw out and develop the strongest aspect of Barth's theological politics – that is, his hopeful confidence in the coming Kingdom of God. Furthermore, what Troeltsch helps one to see is that such hopeful confidence need not devolve into a one-dimensional understanding of the Church's witness; the Church need not constrain the form of its own proclamation to a rigid dogmatic repetition, one that is so preoccupied by the ideal of theological purity that it neglects the virtue of collaboration and the call for faithful compromise. In other words, the Church must remember that it wields no prophetic voice of its own, but only the Word spoken through the Spirit. This is not to say that the Church should be relegated to silence, but rather that it must continue to speak as a witness to the movement of the Spirit. This points the Church towards the option for an "undefensive posture" towards the world, as it listens for the Word that enlivens a future drawn together by the joining of imaginative connections, unforeseen possibilities, and ultimately the widening of a horizon for a new people.[71]

As Hans Joas has shown through his productive engagement with Toeltsch's sociological thought,

> "Troeltsch [...] like few others, rather than seeking to ensure the survival of the Christian faith through withdrawal and isolation, he made [...] an exemplary attempt to think it through afresh in light of the most up-to-date historical research, psychology, sociology, and other sciences."[72]

It is not that Troeltsch was apathetic to the question of Christianity's future, but that Troeltsch was well aware any viable future for Christianity would not be secured by a defensive preservation of a stagnant Christian culture. Ironically, this undefensive posture of Troeltsch's faith leads one back to Barth and the incident at the WCC, since, as Stanley Hauerwas highlights,

> "Barth develops his criticism of the papers prepared for the meeting by observing that many of the documents written for the meeting worry that we may be entering a post-Christian era. Barth challenges that very way of understanding

---

71 Here, my constructive reading of Barth through Troeltsch builds off of Brad East's proposal for a fundamentally undefensive ecclesial posture that he finds in Kathryn Tanner and John Howard Yoder. Brad East, "An Undefensive Presence: The Mission and Identity of the Church in Kathryn Tanner and John Howard Yoder," *Scottish Journal of Theology* 68, no. 3 (July 2015): 337–344.

72 Hans Joas, *Faith as an Option: Possible Futures of Christianity*, trans. Alex Skinner (Stanford, CA: Stanford University Press, 2014), xii.

the task before the church, pointing out the phrase 'post-Christian' was first used by the National Socialists."[73]

In the end, Barth's insistence on the Word of God animated a similar freedom from and for the world that lies at the heart of his positive political theology.

In this key, the prophetic voice of the Church is invoked for the sake of the world, and not as a cudgel against those beyond its walls. Yet, when this latter posture is taken up within the theological political question, as Barth sometimes did, it implicitly assigns the individual theologian with the power of being the sole interpreter of the word of God, a member of the "professorial elite" that stands elevated above and separated from the community of the Church.[74] Certainly, Barth is well aware of such dangers.[75] Yet, as Niebuhr saw, despite his intent to resist these impulses, because Barth so wanted to engage the political question through purely theological pathways, at times his political theology seems to be veiled by an air of transcendent detachment. Regardless, while it may be inevitable that these tendencies will always be lurking in Barth's political thought, this is no reason to leave Barth behind. In fact, perhaps it is with Troeltsch, the unlikeliest of companions, from whom one can draw encouragement to press deeper into the riches of Barth's political theology through a conscious effort to seek the positive role of the Church in the world, but now not only as the inner circle of the State, but also as a member of the wider civil community.

---

73 Hauerwas, "Barth and Reinhold Niebuhr," 637.
74 Sykes, *The Identity of Christianity*, 218–219.
75 Asprey, *Eschatological Presence in Karl Barth's Göttingen Theology*, 14.

Enoch H. Kuo

Theology as Revisionary Political Philosophy
Thinking with Barth on Justification and Justice

> "¹³Then the Pharisees said to him, 'You are testifying on your own behalf; your testimony is not valid.' ¹⁴Jesus answered, 'Even if I testify on my own behalf, my testimony is valid because I know where I have come from and where I am going, but you do not know where I come from or where I am going. ¹⁵You judge by human standards; I judge no one. ¹⁶Yet even if I do judge, my judgment is valid, for it is not I alone who judge but I and the Father who sent me. ¹⁷In your law it is written that the testimony of two witnesses is valid. ¹⁸I testify on my own behalf, and the Father who sent me testifies on my behalf.'" (John 8:13–18, NRSV)

Job's Complaint and the Justice of God

In response to Bildad's defense of God's justice, Job offers a desperate complaint: "How can a mortal be just before God?" (Job 9:2). The normal procedures for seeking justice, Job laments, seem to break down before the face of the divine. As a result, when it comes to God, there is simply no way even to protest one's innocence even if one wanted to. It seems to be impossible to even call into question the divine justice simply on account of the overwhelming wisdom and power that God possesses. In a case of disagreement between mortals, one could appeal to a neutral third party who would be able to adjudicate between the two. But God "is not a mortal, as I am, that I might answer him, that we should come to trial together. There is no mediator between us, who might lay his hand on us both" (Job 9:32–33). And in lieu of a neutral judge to whom one could appeal, one is stuck appealing to the very one whose justice one is attempting to call into question, whose overwhelming superiority in power and wisdom would make such an appeal futile: "If it is a contest of strength, he is the strong one! If it is a matter of justice, who can summon him?" (Job 9:19).

Job 9 finds the eponymous character running into the limits of one of the foundational principles of modern political theory, that *Nemo judex in*

Theology as Revisionary Political Philosophy 137

causa sua – no one can be a judge in their own case – when it comes to the divine-human relation. The principle is all but taken for granted throughout the history of political thought, with figures such as Hobbes, Locke, Rousseau, and Kant all taking it as obvious that the possibility of justice requires the designation of a (sovereign) body who transcends the particular interests of those they judge. For Hobbes, "Where there is no common power, there is no law; where no law, no injustice."[1] For Locke, "Civil Government is the proper Remedy for the Inconveniences of the State of Nature [...] where Men may be Judges in their own Case."[2] For Kant, a condition in which there is "no judge competent to render a verdict having rightful force" between individuals would be a "a state devoid of justice" to be remedied by forcefully compelling those individuals into a state where there can be such a judge if necessary.[3] Indeed, that conflicts are to be resolved by appeal to an

---

1 "To this war of every man against every man, this also is consequent: that nothing can be unjust. The notions of right and wrong, justice and injustice, have there no place. Where there is no common power, there is no law; where no law, no injustice" (Thomas Hobbes, *Leviathan*, ed. Edwin Curley [Indianapolis, IN: Hackett Publishing Company, 1994], XIII.13, 78). See also: "For if we could suppose a great multitude of men to consent in the observation of justice and other laws of nature without a common power to keep them all in awe, we might as well suppose all mankind to do the same; and then there neither would be, nor need to be, any civil government or commonwealth at all, because there would be peace without subjection" (Hobbes, *Leviathan* XVII.4, 107).

2 In Locke's *Second Treatise*: "To this strange Doctrine, viz. That *in the State of Nature, every one has the Executive Power* of the Law of Nature, I doubt not but it will be objected, That it is unreasonable for Men to be Judges in their own Cases, that Self-love will make Men partial to themselves and their Friends. [...] I easily grant, that *Civil Government* is the proper Remedy for the Inconveniences of the State of Nature, which must certainly be Great, where Men may be Judges in their own Case, since 'tis easily to be imagined, that he who was so unjust as to do his Brother an Injury, will scarce be so just as to condemn himself for it: But I shall desire those who make this Objection, to remember that *Absolute Monarchs* are but Men, and if Government is to be that Remedy of those Evils, which necessarily follow from Mens being Judges in their own Cases, and the State of Nature is therefore not to be endured, I desire to know what kind of Government that is, and how much better it is than the State of Nature, where one Man commanding a multitude, has the Liberty to be Judge in his own Case, and may do to all his Subjects whatever he pleases, without the least liberty to any one to question or controle those who Execute his Pleasure?" (John Locke, *Two Treatises of Government* [Cambridge: Cambridge University Press, 1988], ii.13, 275–276).

3 "It is true that the state of nature need not, just because it is natural, be a state of *injustice*, of dealing with one another only in terms of the degree of force each has. But it would still be a state *devoid of justice*, in which when rights are *in dispute*, there would be no judge competent to render a verdict having rightful force. Hence each may impel the other by

agreed-upon third party often plays the key role in differentiating the "state of nature" (where there is no judge and everyone is permitted to enforce their own justice by force) from the "civil condition" (where there is a recognized party to adjudicate disagreements and who possesses sufficient power to enforce their decisions).[4] Job's complaint would seem to call into question the possibility of justice altogether by suggesting that the God-human relation fails to meet the conditions for justice in either a civil (there is no one capable of serving as a mediator between a human being and God) or natural condition (there is no human who could successfully enforce their claims by force or by persuasion against God).

In the face of this difficulty, one might be tempted to qualify the principle by insisting that it is simply improper to apply it to God. What pertains to human-human relationships, one might say, ought not to pertain to the God-human relationship. Indeed, one could see Luther making precisely such a move when he insists in his 1535 *Lectures on Galatians* on a sharp distinction between theology and philosophy when discussing the difference between divine justification and natural justice.[5] Side-stepping Aristotle-in-

---

force to leave this state and enter into a rightful condition" Immanuel Kant, "The Metaphysics of Morals," in *Practical Philosophy*, trans. Mary Gregor [Cambridge: Cambridge University Press, 1996], 456). See also: "Now, a unilateral will cannot serve as a coercive law for everyone with regard to possession that is external and therefore contingent, since that would infringe upon freedom in accordance with universal laws. So it is only a will putting everyone under obligation, hence only a collective general (common) and powerful will, that can provide everyone this assurance. But the condition of being under a general external (i.e., public) lawgiving accompanied with power is the civil condition" (Kant, "The Metaphysics of Morals," 409).

4 Apart from the above, see also Bk.1 ch.6 of Rousseau's *Social Contract*: "For if some rights remained with private individuals, in the absence of any common superior who could decide between them and the public, each person would eventually claim to be his own judge in all things, since he is on some particular point his own judge. The state of nature would subsist and the association would necessarily become tyrannical or hollow." (Jean Jacques Rousseau, *The Basic Political Writings*, 2nd Ed., trans. and ed. Donald A. Cress [Indianapolis, IN: Hackett, 2011], 164.

5 This nexus of connections comes out strongly in Luther's exposition of Galatians 3:10. Luther begins his commentary with emphasizing how important it was to distinguish sharply between a "philosophical" understanding of "doing" and "working" from a "theological" understanding of it: "For in theology those who have been made righteous do righteous things, not as in philosophy, where those who do righteous things are made righteous." Luther then insists that a failure to make this distinction is reflected in how "the sophists, as well as anyone else who does not grasp the doctrine of justification" are able to "snatch the words 'do,' 'work,' and the like, from moral philosophy and from the

spired accounts of justice as a virtue (whether natural or infused) both allowed Luther to continue to insist on the importance of the natural virtues while denying their applicability for understanding the justification of the unjust.[6] Luther's strategy may have created the space for the development of a new "relational" account of justice grounded in faith and the external righteousness of Christ that sought to more adequately capture Pauline and Augustinian soteriological insights, but it does not provide much in the way of an answer to Job's question.

Indeed, Luther's focus on the justification of the sinner may actually have caused him to sidestep the question of whether or not God is just in doing so that is just as much a part of Paul's concern when presenting his gospel to the Romans: "He did this to show his righteousness, because in his divine forbearance he had passed over the sins previously committed; it was to prove at the present time *that he himself is righteous* and that he justifies the one who has faith in Jesus [emphasis mine]" (Rom 3:25–26). Luther's breakthrough famously proposed that one should understand Paul's references to the "righteousness of God" as referring, *not* to the justice by which God would justly judge the unjust (which had caused Luther so much terror), but to "that righteousness which he imparts in order to make men righteous."[7] Yet in its immediate context, it would seem that it is *precisely* the

---

Law, and transfer them to theology." Properly making the distinction, on the other hand, would result in a view that recognized that "'doing' is always understood in theology as doing with faith [...] because in theology we have no right reason and good will except faith." The faculty psychology of the Scholastics remains, but a new distinction between "philosophy" and "theology" now distinguishes between a philosophical kind of "doing" that merely requires right reason and a good will and a theological kind of "doing" that has right reason and good will because of faith. Martin Luther, "Lectures on Galatians 1535: Chapters 1–4," in *Luther's Works*, Vol. 26, ed. Jaroslav Pelikan and Helmut T. Lehman (St. Louis, MO: Concordia, 1955–86), 260–262.

6 Justin Nickel, for instance, has highlighted the ongoing significance of the natural virtues in Luther's thoughts through a study of Luther's sermons. See Justin Nickel, *The Work of Faith: Divine Grace and Human Agency in Martin Luther's Preaching* (Lanham, MD: Lexington Books/Fortress Academic, 2020).

7 Luther on Romans 1:16, "Here, too, *"the righteousness of God"* must not be understood as that righteousness by which he is righteous in himself, but as that righteousness by which we are made righteous (justified) by Him, and this happens through faith in the gospel [...]. The righteousness of God must be distinguished from the righteousness of men which comes from works—as Aristotle in the third chapter of his *Ethics* clearly indicates. According to him, righteousness follows upon and flows from actions. But, according to God, righteousness precedes works and works result from it" (Martin Luther, *Lectures on*

question of God's worthiness to judge, given the fact that he had passed over past sins, that is at stake. Paul approaches the question from a different angle than Job – God's failure to condemn past evils as opposed to God's apparent condemnation of an innocent man – but the question of the justice of God's judgment remains what is at issue.

For Luther, as with much of the tradition before and after him, the transcendence of God would seem to preclude any attempt to question the divine justice. By virtue of being the being of beings, God's justice *in Godself* is precisely that which is inviolable and beyond question. There is no reason to ask whether or not it violates justice for God to be the judge in his own case precisely because there can be no situation in which God could ever be seen as somehow standing in a relation vis-à-vis creation that would make it a relevant question. God is just, that is just what it means for God to be God. To imagine otherwise would seem to be absurd. It is Job's companions, not Job himself, who are in lockstep with the tradition on this point.[8]

There are a few reasons to be dissatisfied with this approach. For one, it leaves Job's query unanswered. That God vindicates Job in the end (even if he does confess that he spoke without knowledge) and that Paul can insist that the gospel manifests – not just the justification of the unjust, but – the justice of God suggests that it may not be wholly inappropriate to call God's justice

---

Romans, ed. and trans. Wilhelm Pauck [Louisville, KY: Westminster John Knox Press, 1961], 18). This interpretation is then used to interpret 3:25–6: "Then, too, the text shows clearly that the apostle calls God righteous because he justifies or makes righteous, as we have stated before. And so it is plainly evident, and this is supported by the apostle as he explains his own words, that 'the righteousness of God' *is* that righteousness by which he makes us righteous, just as the wisdom of God is that by which he makes us wise" (Luther, *Lectures on Romans*, 116–117).

8 Consider, for instance, Thomas Aquinas' commentary on the relevant section of Job 9. The purpose of Job's discourse, Thomas argues, is to show the depth of the wisdom and power of God, against which humans cannot argue: "He shows as a consequence that man cannot approach God in any proportion in arguing a case when he says, "He (God) is wise in heart and Almighty in power." For there are two types of dispute. There is one in which the dispute is carried on by argument and this is done by wisdom. There is another when the dispute is carried on by force and this depends on power. In both of these, God exceeds man, because in both his strength and wisdom he exceeds all strength and wisdom. Consequently he shows both of these pre-eminences. […] Thus, an evident sign that the strength of God exceeds all human strength is the fact that no one can have peace with him by resisting him, but only by obeying him humbly" (Thomas Aquinas, *Commentary on the Book of Job*, trans. Brian Mulladay, www.opwest.org/Archive/2002/Book_of_Job/tajob.html, ch. 9).

Theology as Revisionary Political Philosophy

into question without being impious. What is at stake in the gospel proclamation is not merely the salvation of sinners, but also whether or not God really is just. Indeed, Luther's side-stepping of this question has long been the object of Roman Catholic pushback against the Reformation doctrine of justification. God may exemplify his justice in vindicating the innocent Christ via resurrection, but insisting that he would similarly vindicate sinners who do not possess the inner habitus of graciously infused justice on the basis of a forensic declaration would seem to make God a liar willing to call unjust things just.[9] Insisting that references to the righteousness of God ought *not* to respond to concerns of theodicy but only to the righteousness by which the sinner is to be justified only seems to side-step the question.[10]

Secondly, the insistence on God's unique irreproachability has not remained within the theological sphere, but has also been transferred to talk about human politics. The post-Reformation era, for instance, has slowly seen the appropriation of the notion of sovereignty for political use, a subject most recently catapulted back into conversation through the revival of interest in the work of Carl Schmitt.[11] The concept plays an important role in many classical theorists of the social contract: the formation of a sovereign power is posited as providing the conditions of possibility for inter-human justice, but often comes alongside a claim about the irreproachability of that sovereign.

Take, for instance, Kant's formulation in his mature *Metaphysics of Morals*. Beginning with something akin to the principle *Nemo judex in causa sua*, Kant concludes that the only way for justice to be made possible is for individuals to leave the state of nature (where they are unilaterally their own judges) by uniting themselves into a civil society under the rule of a sovereign power who can represent an "omni-lateral will". Because it is obedience to this sovereign that makes justice possible, one cannot call into question its judgments. Kant makes the parallel to the divine case explicit:

---

9   See canon 11 of the Council of Trent.
10 The traditional Protestant response, of course, has always been to stress that believers are united to Christ by faith such that Christ's righteousness is imputed to them as their own. The Reformed tradition would famously work out this insight in the terms of a theology of covenant. This has not resulted, however, in a broader reevaluation of how justice might be understood philosophically.
11 See Carl Schmitt, *Political Theology: Four Chapters on the Concept of Sovereignty*, trans. George Schwab (Chicago, IL: The University of Chicago Press, 2006).

"For, since a people must be regarded as already united under a general legislative will in order to judge with rightful force about the supreme authority (*summum imperium*), it cannot and may not judge otherwise than as the present head of state (*summus imperans*) wills it to [...]. A law that is law that is so holy (inviolable) that it is already a crime even to call it in doubt in a practical way, and so to suspend its effect for a moment, is thought as if it must have arisen not from human beings but from some highest, flawless lawgiver; and that is what the saying 'All authority is from God' means. This saying is not an assertion about the historical basis of the civil constitution; it instead sets forth an idea as a practical principle of reason: the principle that the presently existing legislative authority ought to be obeyed, whatever its origin."[12]

The laws of the sovereign are to be thought of as divine laws, inviolable, by virtue of the fact that it is only by means of the sovereign that one escapes the problem of always having to be one's own judge in the first place.[13]

The adoption of this principle in modern political theory has not been without its critics. While Kant and many other modern theorists of politics have seen sovereignty as compatible with either democratic, aristocratic, or monarchical governments, a few dissidents have taken the monarchical form to be ineligible on the basis that this would be an unacceptable usurpation

---

12 Immanuel Kant, *The Metaphysics of Morals*, 461–462. See also: "The legislative authority can belong only to the united will of the people. For since all right is to proceed from it, it *cannot* do anyone wrong by its law" (Kant, *The Metaphysics of Morals*, 457).

13 Even Locke, who is often seen as opposing absolute government, nevertheless has a version of this point. Unlike Kant, Locke permits for questioning, but nevertheless acknowledges no concrete recourse by virtue of the lack of a mediator. "The old Question will be asked in this matter of *Prerogative*, But *who shall be Judge* when this Power is made a right use of? I Answer: Between an Executive Power in being, with such a prerogative, and a Legislative that depends upon his will for their convening, there can be no *Judge on Earth*: As there can be none, between the Legislative, and the People, should either the Executive, or the Legislative, when they have got the Power in their hands, design, or go about to enslave, or destroy them. The people have no other remedy in this, as in all other cases where they have no Judge on Earth, but to *appeal to Heaven*" (Locke, *Two Treatises of Government*, xiv.168, 379). "If a Controversie arise betwixt a Prince and some of the People, in a matter where the Law is silent, or doubtful, and the thing be of great Consequence, I should think the proper *Umpire* in such a Case, should be the Body of the *People*. [...] But if the Prince, or whoever they be in the Administration, decline that way of Determination, the Appeal then lies no where but to Heaven. Force between either Persons, who have no known Superiour on Earth, or which permits no Appeal to a Judge on Earth, being properly a state of War, wherein the Appeal lies only to Heaven, and in that State the *injured Party must judge* for himself, when he will think fit to make use of that Appeal, and put himself upon it" (Locke, *Two Treatises of Government*, xix.242).

of God's right to alone remain unquestioned.[14] Thus, John Milton can openly advocate for tyrannicide and republics as the sole appropriate human form of government in England while denying Satan's right to rebel against God on the basis that the republican arguments that work against human monarchs simply do not work against God. Humans are given dominion over creation, but not over one another; dominion over humans belongs to God alone.[15] This partial limitation of sovereignty to republican governments thus opposes the extension of the principle to human politics on the basis that God alone remains irreproachable.

There is a great deal in favor of the traditional settlement, both theologically and politically, but in what follows, I wish to explore the possibility of taking more seriously the challenge that Job 9 offers. In doing so, it is important to note that I am *not* attempting in any way to subordinate theology to philosophy or undermine the Scriptural witness. Rather, it is precisely in taking the witness of the Scriptures seriously that this essay hopes to illuminate new insights that can help one make better sense of *both* one's theological claims and political philosophical commitments alike. This is not the natural theology or ethics to which Barth famously proclaimed his "No!", but closer to the approach that medieval philosophers took vis-à-vis Aristotle or the vision of "theology as revisionist metaphysics" for which Robert W. Jenson called.[16] Just as beliefs about the Trinity, sin, the incarnation, the eucharist, the resurrection of the body, and the final judgment would lead the medieval Scholastics to radically modify and transform the way in which Aristotle's physics and metaphysics were understood, so also the doctrine of justification can transform one's understanding of the nature of justice. An enterprise that took place primarily at the register of epistemology and metaphysics ought also to be expanded to the realm of political theory.

What might such a revisioning look like? Given how deep the respective theological and political issues are, I propose to start the conversation by considering two possibilities: one more "conservative" option and a second more "radical" option. The first option holds that God *does* submit to the principle *Nemo judex in causa sua*. It reads the incarnation and passion nar-

---

14 Eric Nelson has tracked the origins and development of this tradition of thought in Eric Nelson, *The Hebrew Republic: Jewish Sources and the Transformation of European Political Thought* (Cambridge, MA: Harvard University Press, 2011).
15 See John Milton, *Paradise Lost*, XII.33–39 and 65–74.
16 See Robert W. Jenson, *Theology as Revisionary Metaphysics: Essays on God and Creation*, ed. Stephen John Wright (Eugene, OR: Cascade Books, 2014).

ratives as describing in part the ways in which God accommodates to the principle such that it is possible for a third person to serve as a judge between God and his people – the governor Pilate. The significance of Pilate is that he declares Christ innocent in the face of his condemnation by the Jewish authorities, vindicating God in his dispute with his people over the character of covenant faithfulness. In this view, God's self-emptying act of giving up the divine majesty in order to be able to be subject to both the power and wisdom of a human judge is what addresses Job's complaint.

The second option considers the possibility that the principle *Nemo judex in causa sua* is not as universal as often assumed and that it *is* possible for justice to be achieved in a dispute between two parties at odds with one another without appeal to an external third party. It reads the incarnation and passion narratives as describing the ways in which God creates the conditions under which the other parties – Gentile and Jewish alike – are brought to recognition of their sinfulness in the face of divine justice in the way that they are brought to condemn themselves by their own judgments. In this reading, it is less the incarnation itself, but Jesus' actions – especially his submission to abuse and refusal to advocate for himself when brought to trial – that bring to light the emptiness of *both* the judgment of Pilate (as the representative of the Gentiles) and the Sanhedrin (as the representative of the Jews) alike. On this reading, one can side-step the need for a third-party judge by having one party willingly submit without protest to the judgment of the other so as to allow the self-contradictions of the other's position to make itself manifest and allow for self-condemnation. The insistence of the gospel narratives that "the judgment you give will be the judgment you get, and the measure you give will be the measure you get" (Matthew 7:2) thus takes central importance.

The "Conservative" Reading

As it turns out, the first "conservative" option resembles the interpretation offered by Karl Barth in his essay "Justification and Justice" – though, in typical dialectical style, Barth both affirms and denies the significance of the third-party mediator at one and the same time.[17] The essay opens with the broaching of the question of whether or not there is a *positive* relation be-

---

17   The lecture can be found published under the title "Church and State" in Karl Barth, *Community, State, and Church: Three Essays* (Eugene, OR: Wipf & Stock Publishers, 1960).

tween the question of the divine justification of the sinner and the justice of human law, with Barth suggesting that the tradition did not offer much guidance on the matter. Taking inspiration from K.L. Schmidt's lecture on the church-state relation, Barth then launches into a creative interpretation of the significance of Pilate for understanding the relationship between divine and human justice, suggesting that he is "the middleman who takes Him [Jesus] over in the name of paganism, who in so doing declares the solidarity of paganism with the sin of Israel, but in so doing also enters into the inheritance of the promise made to Israel."[18] Barth then simultaneously affirms both the positive role that Pilate, as the representative of the "state", possesses in the passion drama and the negative way in which he plays the role. On the one hand, Pilate is the one who has genuinely been given authority by God to judge Jesus in his contention with the Jews; on the other, he is a symbol of the "demonic" character of the state when it fails to live up to its divine calling. Barth's dialectical interpretation of the trial before Pilate thus would seem to affirm the principle *Nemo judex in causa sua* even as it seeks to negate its significance in the face of the divine judgment on human sinfulness. In the dispute between God and his people, it is significant that the authoritative third party – Pilate – is able to reach the conclusion that Jesus is "innocent", even if he does not ultimately act upon this judgment.[19] It is by appeal to the rulers of the nations that Job's problem of mediation is resolved.

---

18 Barth, *Community, State, and Church*, 111.
19 By contrast, consider Giorgio Agamben's reading of the encounter, which insists on the fact that neither Pilate or Jesus ultimately advance a judgment on the basis that human justice and divine justification cannot meet and must each reciprocally negate themselves in the face of one another. "To testify to the truth, Jesus must affirm and, at the same time, deny his kingdom, which is far away ('it is not from this world') and, at the same time, the very closest, indeed, at hand (entos humōn; Luke 17:21). From the point of view of law his testimony can only fail and end in a farce: the purple robe, the crown of thorns, the reed for a scepter, the screaming: 'Judge!' He — who has not come to judge the world but to save it — finds himself, perhaps precisely for this reason, having to respond in a trial, to submit to a judgment, which his alter ego, Pilate, in the end will not pronounce, cannot pronounce. Justice and salvation cannot be reconciled; every time, they return to mutually excluding and calling for each other. Judgment is implacable and at the same time impossible, because in it things appear as lost and unsavable; salvation is merciful and nevertheless ineffective, because in it things appear as unjudgable. For this reason, on the 'Stone Pavement' called Gabbatha in Hebrew, neither judgment nor salvation—at least as far as Pilate is concerned—take place: they end up in a common, indecisive, and undecidable *non liquet*" (Giorgio Agamben, *Pilate and Jesus*, trans. Adam Kotsko [Stanford, CA: Stanford University Press, 2015], 44–45). In the face of this (double) negative reading, the

Stated more formally, the contest between Job and God can be reframed into one between God and his people more broadly. At stake is the proper understanding of what is just (and therefore who is acting justly). More specifically, the contest concerns the proper interpretation of the Law, which has been entrusted to Israel according to the flesh. If we are to follow Pauline lines, what is to be shown in the revelation of the gospel is not only that God is in the right, but that the failure of the Jews is not to be accounted to a defect in the laws, but to something else. As Paul wrote: "through the law comes the knowledge of sin" (Rom 3:20). Whether it is God in Jesus who is in the right (and thus the leaders of the Jews who are sinning and in the wrong) or whether it is the leaders of the Jews who are in the right and Jesus who is a sinner in the wrong is to be resolved in this first "conservative" reading by appeal to a third party who can be recognized as standing over both. Jesus' willingness to both recognize and submit to the authority of Pilate and Pilate's recognition of Jesus' innocence are thus the key moments which make it possible for God's justice to be vindicated over and against his (Jewish) critics. This particular dynamic of justice and justification is to be replicated among Christ's disciples as they, in turn, are "dragged before governors and kings because of me, as a testimony to them and the Gentiles" (Matt 10:18).[20] It is the rulers of the nations who will play the role of the judge between God and Israel according to the flesh as to which is actually in the right. The God-given power of the statesman, Barth writes, is the "human created instrument of that justification of sinful man that was completed once for all time through that very crucifixion."[21]

This "Barthian" reading of the passion narratives thus preserves the principle *Nemo judex in causa sua* by naming the Gentile ruler the third-party who has been given the authority to judge between God and human. Yet, there is something dissatisfying in the way in which it makes Pilate's (non-) declaration of innocence the key point on which the narrative turns. For one, as Barth himself notes, Pilate's opinion of Christ's innocence did not go so as far as to publically vindicate him against his enemies. Jesus was still scourged and crucified. In Barth's words, the state exercised its power "demonically." Whatever Pilate may have said or thought, his actions certainly seemed to re-

---

positivity of Pilate's declaration of "innocent" in Barth's reading is especially highlighted. Agamben's ultimate denial of any mediation between the divine and the human stands starkly against Barth's willingness to see a determinate role for the state.

20 See also Luke 21:12.
21 Barth, "Church and State," 110.

flect a judgment that was willing to see Jesus put to death. As such, the apostolic witness seems to place the moment of Christ's vindication *not* in the hands of Pilate, but in Christ's resurrection from the dead. As Peter preached on Pentecost: "this man, handed over to you according to the definite plan and foreknowledge of God, you crucified and killed by the hands of those outside the law. But God raised him up" (Acts 1:23–24). But if the Father's exercise of resurrection power is the moment of vindication and judgment, it would seem to nullify the role of the (failed) third party mediator.

Secondly, this reading has a hard time making sense of Jesus' behavior over the course of the trial. The Scriptural witness consistently depicts Jesus as not making much of an effort to defend himself against false testimony, instead responding that it was his interlocutors, and not himself, who were making the (ironic) ascriptions of his kingship and divinity.[22] In order for Pilate to serve as a third party mediator between God and Israel, it would seem to be sufficient that God limit the divine wisdom and power (via incarnation) to that of a human who could be subject to the Gentile ruler. To go to the extent of not even making even a minimal defense so that Pilate could make an informed judgment would seem to go too far.[23] Indeed, there is much in the gospels which would suggest that what took place is less the enactment of the formal mechanisms of justice and more its failure, a lynching rather than a trial.[24]

The "Radical" Reading

These details lead us to consider a different, more "radical" reading of the passion narrative, one which rejects a straightforward reading of the principle *Nemo judex causa sua* in the face of revelation. How can it be possible for a conflict between two parties to be resolved justly without the intervention of a third-party mediator, a situation made more complex by the existence of a massive power-differential between the parties? Jesus' actions during the two trials – before the Sanhedrin and before Pilate – suggest a solution: the spirit of the principle can be maintained in the absence of a third-party by one's willingness to submit to the (incorrect) judgment of the other so as

---

22 Consider, for instance, Matthew 26:64, 27:11; Mark 15:2; Luke 22:70, 23:3; John 18:34, 37.
23 Some, of course, have interpreted Jesus' very presence itself as a kind of "argument" in response to Pilate's question "what is truth?" in John 18:38.
24 John's Gospel narrative seems to portray the passion in this way, with most of the trial happening by insinuation and no actual charges given, i.e., John 18:30.

to allow the other to condemn themselves when they recognize the insufficiencies and self-contradictions of their own judgment. On this reading, despite the fact that Jesus quite openly contested and disputed with various interlocutors over the course of his ministry, it is significant that he offers no rebuttal to his accusers when he is brought before a tribunal and submits to their judgment and mistreatment. By not opposing the other's judgment with one's own, one sets up the conditions whereby the other can come to recognize the justice of one's cause by virtue of recognizing the ways in which their own judgment falls short. In an odd way, the heart of the principle that *Nemo judex in causa sua* is maintained in that one *refuses to judge in one's own cause* by simply allowing the other to provide both the standards of judgment and the judgment itself.

It is important that no resistance is offered because it is precisely by the perpetration of *injustice* against oneself that the righteousness of one's cause vis-à-vis the other is made manifest. Indeed, because whether or not the other is just or unjust in their judgment is precisely what is at issue, it is precisely at the points where one disagrees with the other that one must avoid open resistance of the other's actions. It is by actively bearing the other's violence upon oneself that the epistemological work of bringing the other to doubt their own judgment is accomplished. The execution of Jesus upon the cross is thus supposed to represent the solidarity in sin of the Jewish and Gentile authorities respectively as they are allowed to have their way with God. There is, however, no objective judgment about the significance of this act: whether one views it as a justified action by the authorities or as a flagrant injustice is in part the result of whether one has been convinced of Christ's righteousness over and against that of those who tried him, with whom one stands in the solidarity of sin. The standards of judgment that characterize the passion are, on this reading, decidedly *immanent*.

Barth's insistence on the absoluteness of the divine judgment and his embrace of Pilate's role in judgment means that there are aspects of his thought that are fundamentally opposed to this more "radical" reading. At the same time, however, his dialectical "yes" to the "no" gives him room to notice this very dynamic, even as he seeks to deny its radically immanent. Job, Barth argues, can have nothing to say before God because God is always necessarily in the right.[25] But in Christ: "Jesus maintains the right by electing to let Him-

---

25 "Hence the necessary silence of man suffering before Him, not able to plead any right, not able to confront Him with any well-grounded 'Why?', able only as Job finally did to

self be put in the wrong. He speaks for Himself by being silent. He conquers by suffering. Without ceasing to be action, as action in the strongest sense of the word, as the work of God on earth attaining its goal, His action becomes passion."[26] The paradox of the gospel is found in that the Judge finds himself judged.

The immanent principle of judgment at the center of the "radical" reading can be found multiple times in the Scriptural witnesses. In the Sermon on the Mount, Jesus famously tells his followers "Do not judge, so that you may not be judged. For the judgment you give will be the judgment you get, and the measure you give will be the measure you get" (Matt 7:1–2). There, the principle is set out most explicitly, but hints of it can be found in other passages as well. Consider, for instance, the healing of the blind man in John 9, a passage that plays on the motif of blindness to highlight the paradoxical logic of judgment at play in Jesus' ministry:

> "Jesus said, 'I came into this world for judgment so that those who do not see may see, and those who do see may become blind. Some of the Pharisees near him heard this and said to him, 'Surely we are not blind, are we?' Jesus said to

---

submit under his mighty hand – because as the God who has turned in grace to a sinful and therefore a lost people He is always in the right" (Barth, *Church Dogmatics*, vol. IV, part 1, 174).

26 Barth, *CD IV/1*, 238. See also: "Yet the divine benefit consists with merciless clarity in the hard thing that Jesus must and will allow Himself to be the one great sinner among all other me: *quo nullus maior unquam in mundo fuerit* – to be declared to be such by the mouth of every man, and treated as such at the hand of every man, yet not apart from the will of God, not in abrogation of it, but according to its eternal and wise and righteous direction, in fulfilment of the divine judgment on all men. Jesus must and will allow Himself to take the place which is presumably not His but theirs for the sake of righteousness in the supreme sense. This allowing was determined and effected in divine necessity and freedom. It took place when Jesus was sought out and arrested as a malefactor, when He was accused as a blasphemer before the Sanhedrin and as an agitator against Caesar before Pilate, in both cases being prosecuted and found guilty. It took place when He refrained from saving Himself, from proving His innocence, from defending and justifying Himself, from making even the slightest move to evade this prosecution and verdict. It took place when by means of His great silence He confessed eloquently enough that this had to happen, that He must and will allow it to do so. […] We can explain this only if He saw the triumph of His honor as the One sent by God in what happened to Him, in what He had to suffer when He was set in antithesis to all other men as the one great sinner, because He fulfilled the will of God in so doing, because He did what had to be done for them and the world, taking upon Him their sin and in that way taking it away from them" (Barth, *CD IV/1*, 239).

them, 'If you were blind, you would not have sin. But now that you say, 'We see,' your sin remains.'" (John 9:39–41)

Although far more can be said about this passage, at the very least, Jesus makes the unexpected suggestion that it is those who do not judge (the blind) who understand properly, and that those who do judge (those who see) who do not understand. Jesus' declaration that those who do not see *do not have sin* can be understood in lines with the principle of immanent judgment that we have been developing: because they do not judge, they do not offer a standard by which they can condemn themselves. It is precisely those who seek to offer judgment who will be shown to be sinful by Christ's work.

The principle is also picked up in the post-resurrection writings, particularly in the letters of James and Paul. In attempting to correct disputes among believing Christians, James criticizes the act of judgment, suggesting that "Whoever speaks evil against another or judges another speaks evil against the law and judges the law, but if you judge the law, you are not a doer of the law but a judge" (James 4:11). It is the act of judgment or accusation against another that sets one at odds with the one who is "lawgiver and judge who is able to save and destroy" (James 4:12). While one can certainly interpret this along traditional lines as affirming the irreproachability of the divine judgment, these verses also seem amenable to the immanent interpretation: it is by the very act of offering a judgment that you will be able to be held accountable to it and measured according to it as a "judge" rather than a "doer of the law."

Or consider Paul in Romans 14, working out the implications of this approach to judgment and condemnation:

> "Let us therefore no longer pass judgment on one another, but resolve instead never to put a stumbling block or hindrance in the way of a brother or sister. I know and am persuaded in the Lord Jesus that nothing is unclean in itself, but it is unclean for anyone who considers it unclean. […] Hold the conviction that you have as your own before God. Blessed are those who do not condemn themselves because of what they approve. But those who have doubts are condemned if they eat because they do not act from faith, for whatever does not proceed from faith is sin." (Romans 14:13–15, 22–23)

Rather than posit an "objective" divine measure in accordance with which sins will be judged, Paul instead makes the radical proclamation that *nothing is unclean in itself*. Rather, judgment will be in accord with the measure that one sets for oneself. The ethical call, so it seems, is to avoid a kind of self-contradiction in which one will be self-condemned by virtue of not meeting their own standard. Or consider Paul's advice to believers pursuing a lawsuit against one another in the first letter to the Corinthians: to seek third party mediation from among the Gentiles is considered a significant failing. While Paul considers third party mediation from among the believers to be an acceptable alternative, he also considers a different option that gestures towards the principle of immanent judgment: "In fact, to have lawsuits at all with one another is already a defeat for you. Why not rather be wronged? Why not rather be defrauded?" (1 Cor 6:7).

The radicalness of this particular approach to the passions can perhaps be highlighted by setting it in contrast to penal substitutionary models of the atonement, whether of the classical Reformation or Barthian variety.[27] The fundamental assumption behind this approach is that the justice enacted on the cross is the one that corresponds to the divine standard for sin. What Jesus endures is the divine wrath that is justly reserved for human sin, with the key difference being that Jesus, although innocent, suffers it on behalf of sinners. By contrast, what this reading insists is that what is suffered on the cross is not the divine wrath, but *human* wrath.[28] Jesus is "made sin" not in the sense that he is made into a vicarious substitute for human sinfulness, but that he is given over to human judgment, who declare him "sinful" in accordance to their standards, Jew and Gentile alike. The sin that Jesus bears is not the *wrath of God upon sinners* somehow displaced, but the actual consequences of human sinfulness as expressed in their judgments.

The difference between the two interpretations comes out strongly in the classic hymn of the suffering servant in Isaiah 53:

---

27 The fundamental assumption of post-Anselmian theories of satisfaction is that the offence to God's honor or law demands some kind of commensurate response *which is somehow objectively given by God's law or nature*. While this may still be the case, what I am arguing suggests that it is not this standard that actually plays a key role in the passion, as God deliberately sets it aside in order to accept whatever standard of judgment the Jewish leaders saw fit to put in place.

28 This reading thus can agree with feminist and womanist concerns that traditional formulations of penal substitutionary atonement amount to a kind of divine child abuse. At the same time, however, it attempts to retain something of the penal substitutionary logic, in that it emphasizes that the cross is an expression of juridical punishment—just a human rather than a divine one. See Dolores Williams, *Sisters in the Wilderness: The Challenge of Womanist God-Talk* (Maryknoll, NY: Orbis Books, 1993).

"⁴ Surely he has borne our infirmities
and carried our diseases,
Yet we accounted him stricken,
struck down by God, and afflicted.
⁵ But he was wounded for our transgressions,
crushed for our iniquities;
Upon him was the punishment that made us whole,
and by his bruises we are healed." (Isaiah 53:4–5)

The NRSV reflects the traditional interpretation of the passage in translating מִפְּשָׁעֵנוּ and מֵעֲוֹנֹתֵינוּ "*for* our transgressions" and "*for* our iniquities" respectively. The suffering servant is seen as somehow vicariously suffering the consequences of divine wrath in the place of the hymnist. The punishment for the transgressions and iniquities of the hymnist are laid upon the servant.

Yet, as various commentators have noted, it is far from obvious that the preposition מִן should designate a vicarious suffering in accordance with a mysterious substitution rather than a more straightforward causal interpretation: he was wounded "*because of* our transgressions" and crushed "*because of* our iniquities".[29] Here, the emphasis is on the turn that takes place between verse 4 and 5. Although the hymnist *supposed* that the servant was struck down by God, he was *actually* struck down by the hymnist's people themselves, an act that the hymnist now recognizes to be sinful. In other words, the "punishment" that the servant bears is not the divine punishment, but a human one, a human one that is now recognized as reflecting transgression and iniquity.

It goes far beyond the scope of this paper to work out a complete theory of atonement, but I broach the issue in order to illustrate the potentially "radical" *theological* implications of adopting the more "radical" interpretation. The potential *political* philosophical implications are no less radical. At the onset of this paper, I hinted at the significance of something akin to *Nemo judex in causa sua* for the development of modern political philosophy and the necessity of a transition between the state of nature (in which each judge for themselves) and the civil condition (in which mutually recognized mechanisms for the administration of justice exist). In many of these arguments, the need for a third party with sufficient power to adjudicate between disputes underlies the claim that there must be a sovereign power

---

29 This is, for instance, how the translators of the New English Translation approach the text.

(even if democratically conceived) to which citizens must be subject in order to make justice possible. In Kant's political philosophy, for instance, the inviolability of this sovereign legislative power forecloses any justification of resistance to its authority and warrants viewing its laws as akin to those given by an irreproachable God.

If the passion narratives do indeed depict a way to imagine two persons coming to a just consensus without the mediation of a third party, however, it would seem to lay the foundation for principles which would fundamentally undermine many of these derivations of sovereign power.[30] There are, of course, obvious disanalogies between the theological case and more general human-human relationships. Humans, for instance, do not need to become incarnate in order to make themselves capable of being subject to the violence of their enemies. Yet these disanalogies do not disqualify the fundamental relativization of sovereign power that occurs if it is not necessarily always the case that a powerful third-party is required to mediate between conflicting parties. Even if appeal to a third-party mediator remains a pragmatic norm, the existence of alternative possibilities opens the door for fundamental reimaginations of the nature of authority in the modern state.

And even if the "principle of immanent judgment" remains an edge case for situations where third-party mediation cannot be identified, at the very least it undermines arguments against the permissibility of resistance on the basis that the established institutions or the legislation of the sovereign are the only means by which disputes can be resolved. Indeed, one way to work out the political implications of the "radical reading" may be to attempt to offer a slightly different interpretation of the Christian significance of Martin Luther King's tactics of non-violent resistance.[31] Despite a robust appreciation of the right to self-defense in all other contexts, King was adamant that

---

[30] Interestingly enough, Friedrich Schleiermacher's political philosophy already presses in an anti-sovereign direction, insisting that the exercise of state power is to be understood as the product of a cooperative co-action between citizens and magistrate, with "one-sided" actions from either reflective of rebellion and tyranny respectively. He does not, however, does not extend this conception to incorporate the God-human relationship, which he works out in a more traditional way, in terms of a relation of absolute dependence that makes human freedom and dependence possible in the first place. Schleiermacher's theory of representation and republican liberty is explicated in more detail in ch.4 of Enoch H. Kuo, "Beyond Sovereignty: The Political Theology of Friedrich Schleiermacher" Doctoral Dissertation, Princeton University, 2024.

[31] Consider, for instance, "The Power of Nonviolence (1958)" or any of the other twelve essays collected under the heading of "nonviolence" in Martin Luther King, Jr., *A Testament*

non-violent protestors ought to waive that right in the context of non-violent protest. While as a matter of historical genealogy, King may indeed have been inspired by Ghandi's development of *satyagraha*, one can imagine a slightly different justification of the practice grounded more solidly in a reading of the passion narratives.

What then, of Job? On the "conservative" reading, he would still have to wait until a third-party mediator was capable of exercising power and authority over both himself and God. In other words, in traditional fashion, Job can only be read as anticipating the incarnation. But the "radical" reading suggests a different possibility. Although the power-differential means that Job's ultimate capacity to exercise judgment and work violence against God is limited for the most part to verbal abuse, the fact that he is able to genuinely "despise" himself and "repent in dust and ashes" (Job 42:6) at the end suggests that *something* about the encounter allowed for a kind of revelation and reconciliation. Interpreters of Job have long noted that God does not seem to provide a direct answer to Job's objections, instead taking him on a tour of creation and emphasizing the breadth of the divine wisdom and power. While this can be interpreted in terms of an overwhelming display of God's power and wisdom so as to shut Job up, another way to view this would be to emphasize that *God did not attempt to rebut Job's accusations*. Indeed, it would be Job's companions who had attempted to offer a defense of the divine wisdom and power who would be rebuked because they "have not spoken of me what is right, as my servant Job has" (Job 42:7). As the resurrection of Christ is a manifestation of divine power that can only be a vindication in light of the prior passion, perhaps the divine theophany at the end of Job ought similarly to be read as a kind of divine vindication that follows only after the intimate, patient silence of a God who refused to condemn Job for his protests and, in doing so, effects his self-condemnation without a need for a mediator.

---

of Hope: The Essential Writings and Speeches of Martin Luther King, Jr., ed. James Melvin Washington [New York: Harper Collins, 1986].

Rezensionen / Reviews

Rezensionen / Reviews

Michael Weinrich, Die eine heilige christliche und apostolische Kirche. Berufung und Sendung der Gemeinde (Ekklesiologie in reformatorischer Perspektive 1), Göttingen 2023.

M. Weinrich lehrte als Professor für Systematische Theologie an den Universitäten Paderborn, Berlin (FU) und Bochum (dort auch Direktor des Ökumenischen Instituts), wo er 2015 emeritiert wurde. Der hier vorgelegte Band des ev.-reformierten Theologen enthält z.T. überarbeitete Vorträge und Aufsätze sowie Originalbeiträge, die insgesamt eine farbige, stimmige Collage wichtiger Elemente reformatorischer Ekklesiologie darstellen. Die 17 Kapitel gliedert er in Fundamentalorientierungen (Kap. 1–5), klassische Attribute der Kirche (6–9), und Perspektiven (10–16). Am Schluss folgt eine biblische Meditation (17). Die Kapitel des Buches werden hier in Auswahl referiert und am Ende zusammenfassend kommentiert.

Teil I Die Fundamentalorientierungen beginnen im 1. Kapitel mit der Frage:
1. *Welche Kirche meinen wir?* Im Rückblick auf bis heute nachwirkende ekklesiologische Denkfiguren geht W. zunächst auf *Augustins* Vorstellung von der Kirche als *corpus permixtum* ein. Die irdische Kirche umfasst eine menschliche Gemeinschaft, die nicht für sich beanspruchen kann, wahre Kirche zu sein. Vielmehr ist dem Herrn der Kirche das Urteil zu überlassen, wer am Ende als wahrer Christ zu gelten hat und wer nicht (vgl. Jesu Gleichnis vom Unkraut unter dem Weizen, Matth. 13,24–30). Dagegen hat sich die *römisch-katholische* Kirche im Mittelalter immer deutlicher selbst als wahre Kirche und Platzhalterin Christi stilisiert und als *corpus christianum* bezeichnet. Dies führte zum entschiedenen reformatorischen Protest. *Luther* begriff die wahre Kirche als die im Glauben an Gottes Wort versammelte Gemeinde. Sie wird durch das Wirken des Heiligen Geistes konstituiert und bleibt ihrem Wesen nach *verborgen*. Ähnlich verstand auch *Calvin* als „dankbarer Schüler der Theologie Luthers" (S. 46) die Kirche als unsichtbare Einheit der in Christus erwählten Menschen. Allerdings warnt Calvin auch vor der Gefahr einseitiger Betonung der Verborgenheit, nämlich der Gnade Gottes nicht mehr zuzutrauen, sich in der geschichtlichen Gestalt von Kirche bemerkbar zu machen. So entwickelt er später ein Modell der *sichtbaren Gestalt* von Kirche im Zusammenwirken funktional gegliederter Dienste unter der Königsherrschaft Christi.

Vor diesem historischen Hintergrund skizziert W. seine Antwort auf die zu Beginn gestellte Fragen mit einer Reihe von Grundorientierungen. (1)

Die Kirche bleibt in jeder Hinsicht auf Gottes Verheißung angewiesen und ist nur dann wahre Kirche, wenn in ihr die Gegenwart Christi durch das Wirken des Heiligen Geistes erscheint. Dem entspricht sie in der Grundhaltung des Gebetsrufes *Kyrie eleison*. Wenn sie aber der Verheißung Gottes keine präsentische Kraft mehr zutraut, legt sie sich ganz auf die Selbstdarstellung ihrer Defizite fest. So verkommt sie zur Klagegemeinschaft. Dagegen ist die die Möglichkeit offenzuhalten, „dass wir einer Verheißung Gottes mehr zutrauen als unserem empirischen Eindruck" (S. 63) und dementsprechend auch Gott loben und *Halleluja* singen können. (2) In diesem Sinn ist die *Kirche zu glauben*. Gerade als geglaubte Kirche hat sie sich ihre eigene *Weltlichkeit* klar zu machen. Sie ist ganz und gar weltlich und steht in der Welt, aber nicht ihr gegenüber. Ihr Gegenüber ist Gott. (3) Im horizontalen Verhältnis zu den anderen Menschen versteht sich die Kirche im Glauben als *Gemeinschaft der Heiligen*. Es kann sich in diesem Verhältnis nur um eine doppelte Sichtbarkeit halten, die einerseits dem Glauben im Binnenverhältnis mehr zu sehen gibt als es sich andererseits für die Augen der Mitmenschen in der Welt darstellen mag.

    2. *Die Kirche, das Wort Gottes und die Schrift*. Schon der Umfang dieses längsten Kapitels im Buch unterstreicht die besondere ekklesiologische Bedeutung des reformatorischen Schriftprinzips. Die Kirche verdankt ihre Existenz dem Wort Gottes: sie ist creatura verbi divini. Unter Luthers prägendem Einfluss gewinnt der Glaube an die Selbstevidenz der Heiligen Schrift entscheidende Bedeutung für die Theologie, mehr noch: für das Leben in der Kirche mit der Bibel und für die schriftgemäße Verkündigung. Dabei gibt sich die Wahrheit in ihr ohne menschliches Zutun zu erkennen. Es ist dem Wirken des Heiligen Geistes zu verdanken, wenn das in den Schriften des Alten und Neuen Testaments eröffnete Wort Gottes klar und verständlich spricht und von uns Menschen gehört wird. So bleibt es unserem Zugriff entzogen. Selbst dort, wo die Anrede Gottes in direkter erfolgt, wie bei der Gottesbegegnung Moses am Dornbusch (Ex. 3,4ff), ist das Wort Gottes selbst nicht zitierbar. Insofern ist die theologische Rede vom Wort Gottes eine „Metapher dafür, wie Gott sich selbst uns verständlich macht" (Ingolf U. Dalferth, wirkendes Wort S. 281; zitiert nach W. S. 78). Die Kirche ist als „Kirche unter dem Wort" nachgeordnet. Dabei schützt die Differenzierung zwischen der Bibel als Buch und dem in ihr sprechenden Wort Gottes auch vor dem Missverständnis, die Reformation habe die Autorität des Papstes in Rom einfach durch die Bibel als "papieren Papst" ersetzt. Fundamentalistische und biblizistische Auslegungsformen werden insofern abgewehrt, als sich das Wort Gottes

nicht am geschriebenen Buchstaben festmachen lässt, sondern allererst im lebendigen Wirken des Heiligen Geistes zu sprechen beginnt. Dabei tendiert das in den Worten der Bibel aufgeschriebene Wort Gottes von vornherein zur mündlichen Mitteilung in der Predigt. Der Lebendigkeit des Wortes Gottes entspricht die „pünktliche Mündlichkeit der Schrift" (S. 97).

4. *Die Kirche als Volk Gottes an der Seite Israels.* M.E. stellt dieses Kapitel einen der wichtigsten neuen Aspekte der Ekklesiologie Weinrichs dar. Zunächst zeichnet er die historische Entwicklung der Wiederentdeckung des Begriffes „Volk Gottes" seit dem 19. Jahrhundert nach. Der Begriff wurde im Protestantismus auf das (deutsche) Volk im nationalen Sinn als „*Volkskirche*" angewandt. Im NS-Volkswahn wurde dann das Begründungsverhältnis der ursprünglichen Verwendung des Begriffes in der Bibel umgekehrt. Während sich dort Gott sein Volk (Israel) erwählt, so wählt sich nun das (deutsche) Volk seinen Gott. Demgegenüber kam es nach Kriegsende zu einer entscheidenden Wende. Im protestantischen Bereich vollzog sich mit der Gründung des Weltrates der Kirchen ein ökumenischer Aufbruch. Dessen 1. Vollversammlung bekannte 1948 in Amsterdam, dass wir „in Jesus Christus eins sind", nämlich in der Ganzheit der *Gemeinschaft von Amtsträgern und „Laien" als Volk Gottes*, wie in bewusster Anspielung auf das alttestamentliche Zeugnis vom befreienden Handeln Gottes an seinem Volk Israel formuliert wurde. Das Vaticanum II bezeichnet Israel als das erste von Gott erwählte Volk, auf das später die Kirche in einem weiteren Schritt folgt, wenn sie gemeinsam mit Israel „als wanderndes Gottesvolk nach der himmlischen Stadt sucht" (Hebr. 13,14 / lumen gentium 9). Entsprechend bezog später auch *die Theologie der Befreiung in Lateinamerika* das Handeln Gottes dereinst beim Auszug Israels aus Ägypten nun in der Hoffnung auf seinen Beistand für die Leidenden und Entrechteten in ihrem gegenwärtigen Kontext. Schließlich eröffnete der seit den 1960er Jahren entstandene jüdisch-christliche Dialog eine neue Sicht im Verhältnis von Juden und Christen. Seither wurden verschiedene Modelle der Verhältnisbestimmung des alten Volkes Israel zu der Kirche Jesu Christi entwickelt bis hin zu dem von W. favorisierten des *einen Gottesvolkes* aus Juden und Christen.

Dessen einendes Band ist die Treue Gottes, der im Volk Israel wie in der Kirche das Vertrauen auf IHN entspricht, „der Bund und Treue hält ewiglich / und nicht preisgibt das Werk seiner Hände" (vgl. Ps. 146,6, Dtn 7,6–8, Ps. 138,8b), wie es auch die Ev. Kirche der Union im Introitus ihres Gottesdienstes nach Grundform II bekennt (Anm. des Rezensenten). So wie Israel aus Gottes freier Gnade zum Bundespartner erwählt wurde, so wurde danach auch die christliche Kirche zum Mitpartner im selben Bund aufgenommen. Gleichwohl weist W. auf Gottes bleibende Geheimnis in Bezug auf das Verhältnis von Israel und Kirche hin. Christliche Theologie ist an dieser Stelle zur erhöhten Bedachtsamkeit aufgefordert, geht es doch um Gottes ureigene Entscheidung, wenn der Kirche gemeinsam mit Israel die Gnade gewährt wird, als Volk Gottes an der Seite Israels gelten zu dürfen.

5. Im letzten Kapitel seiner Fundamentalorientierungen wendet sich W. dem Thema *Kirche der Freiheit – Freiheit der Kirche* zu. Eingangs geht er auf das Impulspapier der EKD zum Reformprozess (2006) ein. Darin wird Luthers Schrift *Von der Freiheit eines Christenmenschen* zwar „gern zitiert", allerdings „ohne dass etwas von dem zutiefst dialektischen Charakter der hier thematisierten Freiheit auch nur geahnt wird" (S. 176). Tatsächlich aber hat reformatorische Theologie ein durchaus besonderes Verständnis von Freiheit zu profilieren, das sich keineswegs ohne weiteres aus einem allgemeinen Verständnis von Freiheit ableiten lässt. W. grenzt dieses Verständnis von Freiheit gegen die neuzeitliche Vorstellung menschlicher Autonomie ab, die sich der Selbstverwirklichung des Menschen das Doppelgebot der Liebe zu Gott und dem die Bedingungen menschlicher Freiheit selbst setzen zu können meint.

So wird z.B. im Konzept Nächsten um ein Drittgebot erweitert. Dabei erhält die Liebe zu mir selbst ein solch starkes Gewicht, das am Ende alles auf den Spruch hinausläuft: „*Unterm Strich zähl ich*" (S. 184). Die m.E. scharf beobachteten Fehlentwicklungen in dieser Richtung führt Verf. auf ein Freiheitsverständnis zurück, das die Selbstkonstitution des Individuums postuliert. Kants kategorischer Imperativ erscheint demgegenüber rücksichtsvoller, wird doch hier die Freiheit des Einzelnen durch die des Anderen begrenzt; aber dabei kommt der andere nur als Begrenzung meiner selbst in den Blick. Die Begegnung mit dem anderen ist keine Beglückung, sondern meine Freiheit einengende Pflicht (S. 184).

Ganz anders nimmt die Bibel in Gen. 1 den Menschen wahr. Wenn Gott den Menschen (Singular) nach seinem Bilde schafft, dann schafft er zwei: *und er schuf sie als Mann und als Frau (Gen. 1,26)*. Dabei wird nicht auf die Alternative Mann oder Frau abgehoben, sondern auf das Gegenübersein des anderen. Freiheit wird hier als *Freiheit zur Beziehung* verstanden. „Es ist nicht vorgesehen, dass der Mensch mit sich selbst auskommt" (S. 187). „Die *Freiheit der Kirche* wurzelt in dem Lebenshorizont, in dem jeder einzelne von vornherein beziehungsfähig ist [...]. In der Kirche sind die Menschen versammelt, die sich nicht um die ihnen geltende Gnade Gottes

Sorgen machen" (S. 197), sondern im Vertrauen auf Gott zusammenstehen. Wir Menschen sind eben nicht als Wölfe zum Lebenskampf um uns selbst geschaffen, sondern für einander und zum Lobe Gottes und somit zur Freiheit des lebendigen Miteinanders.

In Teil II seines Buches geht W. auf die *Attribute* der Kirche ein (Kap. 6–9), wie sie im ökumenischen Konzil von Nicäa-Konstantinopel 381 in dessen 3. Artikel bekannt worden sind: *Wir glauben an den Heiligen Geist [...] und die eine, heilige, christliche und apostolische Kirche*. Diese Aufzählung ist die im weitesten Sinn ökumenische Beschreibung der Kirche, auf die sich bis heute die ganze Christenheit verständigen kann, wenn auch jede einzelne Kirche den Grundtext je auf ihre Weise auslegt.

6. *Einheit* vollzieht sich in dem aktuellen Hören auf Gottes Wort für unsere Gegenwart und dem ihm entsprechenden neuen *Bekennen* des Glaubens. Es geht dabei um das konfessorische Ereignis bekennender Lebendigkeit, statt um konfessionelle Identität.

7. Die *Heiligkeit* ist nicht aus allgemeinen Phänomenen von Heiligkeit in der religiösen Landschaft abzuleiten, um von da aus so etwas wie besondere „christliche Heiligkeit" zu profilieren; sondern auf der Offenbarung Gottes gründend kann uns Gottes Wort heute so treffen, dass wir dem ganz Anderen begegnen, dem wir in unserer menschlichen Antwort am besten in Ehrfurcht entsprechen. Heiligkeit ist die Weise, in der sich Gott uns nähert und mit uns verbindet, ohne dass die Distanz zwischen ihm und uns aufgegeben wird.

8. Die *Katholizität* der Kirche ist heute vielen evangelischen Christen nicht mehr bewusst, nachdem Luther den Begriff durch *christlich* ersetzt hat, um sein Kirchen-Verständnis von dem der röm.-katholischen Kirche abzugrenzen. W. regt aber an, in der Evangelischen Kirche heute wieder mit der ganzen Christenheit die *katholische* Kirche zu bekennen. Luther und Calvin stimmen diesbezüglich überein. Sie übernehmen die drei traditionellen Kriterien, wonach als katholisch zu gelten habe, was immer, überall und von allen im Glauben bekannt wurde; doch fügen sie noch die Schriftgemäßheit hinzu, denn nur das könne katholisch sein, was nach der Schrift zu belegen ist. Heute besteht Konsens zwischen der röm.-katholischen und den protestantischen Kirchen, dass Katholizität von Gottes Geist ermöglicht wird und nicht von vorherein gegeben ist. Geschenkte Katholizität bringt die Kirchen zueinander, indem sie diese in all ihrer Verschiedenheit mit dem gemeinsamen Zentrum verbindet.

9. Die *Apostolizität* der Kirche betont deren Beziehung zu ihrem Ursprung in der Begegnung der Apostel mit

dem auferstandenen Christus. Zwar hält auch Er Distanz zu den Jüngern. Aber durch den Heiligen Geist werden sie zu Auferstehungszeugen. An dieser Stelle sieht W. eine Brücke zur orthodoxen Kirche, betont doch gerade sie die Wirksamkeit des Geistes am Ursprung als der Kraft, die bis heute in der Kirche wirkt. Allerdings wird die Kontinuität der Apostolizität im protestantischen Bereich weniger durch das Amt (im Sinne ununterbrochen fortgesetzter Amtsnachfolge) garantiert als in kontinuierlicher, schriftgemäßer Verkündigung bezeugt.

In Teil III lenkt W. den Blick auf verschiedene *Perspektiven* unter den zuvor beschriebenen Fundamentalbedingungen und Visionen der den Attributen entsprechenden Kirche.

10. Das Kapitel geht auf einen Vortrag zurück, den W. 2007 in. einem Lehrgespräch zwischen dem Lutherischen und dem Reformierten Weltbund zum Verhältnis von *Tradition und Bekenntnis* gehalten hat. W. konstatiert den weitgehenden Konsens der beiden Kirchen auch in. ihren unterschiedlichen Traditionen und Bekenntnisaussagen aufgrund der alles überwölbenden Übereinstimmung in der Bedeutung des biblischen Zeugnisses. Demgegenüber sollten die verbleibenden Unterschiede nicht überbetont werden, auch wenn sie jeweils wichtige Aspekte der beiden Kirchen betreffen. Dabei geht es in lutherischer Sicht primär um die Soteriologie und dort um die Rechtfertigung allein aus dem Glauben. In reformierter Perspektive geht es vor allem um die Ehre Gottes und erst daraufhin um das Heil der Menschen. Aus dieser Sicht kommt dann auch die Rechtfertigung des Gottlosen in den Blick.

11. *Gerechtfertigt für die Bundespartnerschaft*. Die Bedeutung der Rechtfertigungslehre für das Ganze der Theologie wird in reformierter Sicht deutlicher, wenn sie im Gesamtzusammenhang der Geschichte Gottes mit den Menschen erörtert wird, und d.h. in dem schon in der Schöpfung angelegten Gefälle von Gottes Hinwendung zu den Menschen, mit denen er alsbald ein partnerschaftliches *Bundesverhältnis* eingeht, das ganz und gar auf seinem Treueversprechen gründet.

13. *Die Profanisierung der Bilder*. Das für nicht in reformierter Tradition aufgewachsene Christen (wie den Rezensenten) lehrreiche Kapitel beschäftigt sich mit dem Bilderverbot aus Ex. 20,4–5. Der historische Hintergrund der kultischen Bilderverehrung und die theologischen Motive der reformatorischen Bilderkritik werden überzeugend erläutert. Zwischen Luther, Zwingli und Calvin gab es diesbezüglich keinen Dissens. Innerprotestantische Lehrgegensätze in dieser Hinsicht wurden erst später behauptet. Luther sah in dem Bilderkult ein „Affenspiel" (bei W. S. 316), und umgekehrt war

Calvin kein Bilderfeind. „Das Bild, das Calvin ablehnt, ist nicht das Bild, das Luther erlaubt und wünscht" und das „Bild Christi, das Luther wertvoll war, ist nicht das Bild Christi, das Calvin ablehnt" (M. Stirm, Die Bilderfrage in der Reformation S. 224f; zitiert bei W. S. 322).

14. *Die Wahrheit des Bilderverbots.* In unserem Reden von Gott kommen wir nicht ohne Bilder aus. W. nennt dies die „Notwendigkeit des Unzulänglichen" (S. 337). Im Reden von Gott geht es um die für unser Verstehen notwendigen Wort-Bilder, in denen wir uns Ihn vorstellen, z.B. wie einen Vater, eine Mutter, einen König, usf. Aber sobald wir die Wort-Bilder in Bild-Bildern darstellen, haben wir Gott auf diese bildhaft dargestellte Vorstellung festgelegt. Deshalb vermeidet die Bibel auch in ihrer Rede von Gott, ihre Wort-Bilder mit dem bestimmten Artikel zu versehen. Gott ist nicht *der* Vater, *die* Mutter usf., sondern allenfalls wie *ein* Vater, *eine* Mutter vorstellbar. Das Bilderverbot schützt die unverfügbare Gottesbeziehung davor, dass wir sie in Bild-Bildern zu fixieren versuchen. W. spricht diesbezüglich von der „Notwendigkeit des Unzulänglichen".

So sollen wir uns nicht nur auf die uns gefälligen Aspekte konzentrieren, andere hingegen ausblenden, wie z.B. die biblischen Wort-Bilder vom zornigen oder richtenden Gott. Schließlich gilt das Bilderverbot auch unseren theologischen Lehraussagen, in denen wir mehr über Gott Bescheid zu wissen meinen, als er uns selbst von sich mitgeteilt hat. „Nicht wir ermöglichen Gott sein In-Erscheinung-Treten, sondern es ist Gott, der uns in den Bildern seines Handelns über uns selbst ins Bild setzt. Das ist die Wahrheit des Bilderverbots" (S. 348).

15. *Missio Dei und die Sendung der Kirche.* In seinen Ausführungen zur Missionstheologie bezieht sich W. auf einen frühen Aufsatz von Karl Barth (Die Mission und die Theologie in der Gegenwart, 1932, abgedruckt in: K. Barth, Vorträge und kleinere Arbeiten 1922–1925 [GA III], Zürich 2013 S. 156–208) sowie dessen Ausführungen zur Sendung der Kirche am Ende der Versöhnungslehre seiner Kirchlichen Dogmatik (KD IV/3, vgl. dort S. 40ff, S. 553ff, S. 780ff). Sie orientieren sich an dem theologischen Aufbruch in der Missionstheologie und missionarischen Praxis nach dem Ende des kolonialen Zeitalters unter der programmatischen Übersicht der *Missio Dei* als sowohl bußfertigem Ausdruck der Abkehr von der bisher vorherrschenden Sichtweise (dass „wir" aus den entsendenden Kirchen in Europa und Nordamerika den „Heiden" in den bisherigen Kolonien das Evangelium bringen) zugunsten der neuen Einsicht, dass Gott selber das Subjekt der Mission ist, indem er sein Wort in dre Einen Welt wirken lässt, wann und wo er will. W. bedauert, dass es im englischen Sprachraum

kein Äquivalent für das deutsche Wort *Sendung* gibt, mit dem K. Barth die Mission Gottes und daraufhin den Auftrag der Kirche bedenkt. Dieser Welt ist zunächst zu bezeugen, dass sie keinen Gott hat. Sie hat so in der Welt aufzutreten, dass sie die Existenz der Götter bestreitet, denen die Welt huldigt. Mission ist für Barth Entgötterung der Welt. In ihrem Auftreten in der Welt hat die Kirche nicht auf ihre eigenen. Leuchttürme und Best-Praxis-Beispiele zu verweisen, sondern auf das Licht Gottes, das in dieser Welt leuchtet. Dies bezeugt sie in ihrer Verkündigung und in ihrer Aufmerksamkeit auf die Brennpunkte des Elends: auf Hunger nach Brot und Durst nach Freiheit und Gerechtigkeit, auf Opfer der Kriege und eines ungerechten Weltwirtschaftssystems, ohne dabei die Welt retten zu wollen; denn sie weiß um das vollbrachte Versöhnungswerk Christi. Sie wird aber den Blick der Zeitgenossen auf die nahen und fernen Nächsten in ihren unterschiedlichen Bedrängnissen zu lenken versuchen, denen nach dem Zeugnis der Bibel die besondere Aufmerksamkeit Gottes gilt. Sie wird im Eingeständnis auch der eigenen Bedürftigkeit von Trost und Ermutigung um Glauben an und Vertrauen auf unsere Wahrnehmung der lebendigen Gegenwart Christi in dieser heutigen Welt bitten.

Kommentar

Bekenntnistradition und Zeitgenossenschaft

In seinem Vorwort hatte W. gemutmaßt: „möglicherweise scheint ein erheblicher Teil meiner Überlegungen heute ein wenig aus der Zeit gefallen zu sein" (S. 178). Die Vermutung dürfte für den Teil der theologischen Öffentlichkeit zutreffen, der die Schriften des (von W. mehrfach erwähnten) Theologen Karl Barth wenn überhaupt, dann wenig gelesen hat und in jedem Fall jetzt für überwunden hält. Richtig ist, dass unsere Kirche heute vor anderen Aufgaben steht als seinerzeit die Bekennende Kirche. Aber m.E. versteht es Weinrich, das einst von den theologischen Vorgängern Gesagte auf unsere gegenwärtige Situation zu beziehen. Dabei kommt ihm zugute, dass er zu den (nicht allzu zahlreichen) profunden Kennern der Kirchlichen Dogmatik und ihr vorausgegangener älterer Schriften der dialektischen Theologie Barths zählt, die deren Denkstrukturen so gründlich durchdacht und eigenständig rezipiert haben, dass sie das einstmals von anderen Geschriebene in eigenen Worten und in eigener Verantwortung für unsere heutige Situation in verständlicher Anschaulichkeit neu sagen können.

Christologische Zentrierung und ökumenische Weite

Letzteres trifft insbesondere auf die christologische Orientierung der hier vorgelegten Ekklesiologie in reformatorischer Perspektive zu. Immer wieder spricht W. von der (trinitarisch vermittelten) *Gegenwart des lebendigen Christus,* die der Kirche verheißen ist. Sie ist der Grund der Kirche auf Erden und daraufhin auch Ermöglichung des christlichen Lebens in der Antwort auf das Erscheinen Christi in der Welt. Der christologischen Konzentration auf der einen Seite entspricht als deren Folge die *ökumenische Weite.* Schon die Vielfalt der Adressaten der hier versammelten Vorträge und Aufsätze ist ein Indiz für die Dialogfähigkeit dieser Ekklesiologie. Gerade in der Erkennbarkeit seiner reformierten Herkunft überzeugt m.E., was Weinrich in diesem Band zum innerprotestantischen Verhältnis zwischen Lutheranern und Reformierten beiträgt, deren Gemeinsamkeiten er sowohl im geschichtlichen Rückblick auf Luther und Calvin betont als auch entsprechend in den aktuellen Lehrgesprächen zwischen Lutherischem und Reformiertem Weltbund zur Geltung brachte. Noch bestehende Unterschiede in der evangelischen Konfessionsfamilie sind keine kontroversen Positionen, sondern als unterschiedliche Akzentuierungen und Bereicherung der Vielfalt in der Kirche zu verstehen. – Sodann insistiert W. auf der Katholizität der evangelischen wie der *römisch-katholischen* Kirche und der ganzen Christenheit und entwickelt so Gesprächsfähigkeit mit den Glaubensgeschwistern in Deutschland und in Rom. Einige Beiträge gehen auch auf Gespräche mit der *Anglikanischen Kirche* in der Meißen-Kommission zurück. Schließlich sind die Kapitel über die Attribute der Kirche aus dem Glaubensbekenntnis von Nicäa-Konstantinopel im Zusammenhang mit seiner Mitwirkung am Gespräch der EKD mit der Rumänisch-*Orthodoxen Kirche* entstanden, in dem sich in Weinrichs Interpretation der Apostolizität ein möglicher Brückenschlag zur Orthodoxie eröffnet. Nicht zuletzt wird die Weite dieser Ekklesiologie auch in Weinrichs Bemühen deutlich, sich im Gespräch zwischen *Juden und Christen* in behutsamer Annäherung als unterschiedliche Partner des einen Bundes mit Gott und als Glieder des einen Gottesvolkes zu entdecken, um sich so auf den Weg und die Suche nach der bleibenden Stadt zu machen.

Bescheidenheit und Kompromisslosigkeit

Theologische Existenz bewegt sich zwischen Bedürftigkeit und Anspruch. Bei der Lektüre des Buches beeindruckt einerseits Weinrichs durchgehend *nüchterne und realistische Sicht der Welt,* in der Kirche lebt und deren Teil sie ist; andererseits, und zwar nicht im paradoxalen Gegensatz, sondern in Entsprechung zu dieser realistischen Sicht, klingt bei W. auch immer wieder der zuversichtliche Grundton an, wenn er von Gottes Treue, von der auf der Kirche liegenden Verheißung bzw. der ihr in Aussicht gestellten Gegenwart des lebendigen Christus spricht. Insofern ist dieses Buch auch zum *Trost und zur Ermutigung* für Christen in den Gemeinden mit deren Pfarrerinnen und Pfarrern geschrieben, die an ihren Aufgaben in der Welt von heute oft genug zu verzagen drohen. Dabei bleibt Verf. sich durchgehend der Gefahr bewusst, dass wir Theologen den Mund zu voll nehmen könnten; denn nach wie vor gilt die Einsicht des jungen Karl Barth, dass wir zwar von Gott reden wollen und sollen, dass wir aber nicht von Gott reden können. Wir sind und bleiben darauf angewiesen, dass Gott selbst zu uns redet und also seinen Heiligen Geist wirken lässt. Immer wieder mahnt W. deshalb zur *Bescheidenheit.* Nun ist das mit der Bescheidenheit in Theologie und Kirche so eine Sache. Zu oft erwies sich der moralische Imperativ als verdecktes Herrschaftsmittel; und von ihrem Ziel her ist die hier vorgestellte Ekklesiologie eher anspruchsvoll als bescheiden. Jedoch gibt ein früheres Buch von W. einen Wink, wo es im Titel heißt: „Die bescheidene Kompromisslosigkeit der Theologie Karl Barths". Darum geht es W. auch im hier besprochenen Buch. Die Theologie hat die falschen Götter dieser Welt mutig und kompromisslos zu bekämpfen. Das ist ihr theologischer Anspruch. Jedoch darf sie nie die Grenze ihrer eigenen Möglichkeiten aus dem Auge verlieren; insofern hat jeder einzelne in seiner kirchlichen und theologischen Existenz bescheiden zu bleiben, als all seine noch so wohl durchdachten Sätze der Bewahrheitung durch Gott selber bedürfen. Kyrie eleison!

Insgesamt ist es Weinrich gelungen, die aus sehr unterschiedlichen Situationen entstandenen Gelegenheitsbeiträge in einem klar geordneten Ganzen zu strukturieren. So entspricht er auch dem selbst verordneten Anspruch „pünktlicher Katholizität", nämlich Kontextualität und Allgemeinheit theologischer Aussagen zusammen zu denken. Jedenfalls bedient W. nicht das verbreitete Vorurteil von der Ferne dogmatisch-theologischer Aussagen gegenüber dem, was hier und heute theologisch dran ist. Dem Rezensenten ist es bei der Lektüre oft so ergangen wie in früheren Jahren, wenn er an einem der jährlich von W. angebotenen Pastoralkollegs in Westfalen teilnahm. Zu Beginn hielt er einen stets sorgfältig vorbereiteten und zum Gespräch anregenden Vortrag. Aber dann ließ uns der Professor nicht wie sonst oft üblich nach kurzer „Aussprache" mehr oder weniger beeindruckt zurück, sondern blieb noch die ganze Woche als aufmerksamer Zuhörer und Gesprächspartner

Rezensionen / Reviews

bei uns, wenn unsere Probleme und Schwierigkeiten im pastoralen Alltag zur Sprache kamen. Ich war sicher nicht der einzige unter den Teilnehmenden, der am Ende ermutigt und gestärkt nach Hause fuhr, weil mir neu klar geworden war, wozu ich eigentlich Pfarrer geworden bin.

Zum Schluss blickt W. „statt eines Nachworts" in einer biblischen Meditation auf den Anfang zurück. Er lädt seine Leserschaft ein, sich zu Füßen des Evangelisten Lukas zu setzen und ihm zuzuhören, was er über *das Geheimnis der Kirche* zu erzählen hat. Da hören wir von zwei namentlich unbekannten Männern, die aus Enttäuschung über die Ereignisse in Jerusalem die Gemeinschaft mit den anderen Jüngern verlassen hatten. So sind sie nun auf dem Weg zurück in das alte Leben vor ihrer gemeinsamen Zeit mit Jesus. Da begegnet ihnen ein unbekannter Dritter. Dieser nimmt ihre trostlose Traurigkeit wahr.

Er legt ihnen nun aus, was die Schriften über den Christus sagen. Am Abend der Ankunft in Emmaus laden die beiden den Unbekannten zum Mahl ein. Über dem Brechen des Brotes bei Tische gehen ihnen die Augen in dem Moment auf, als der Fremde vor ihren Augen verschwindet. *„Brannte nicht unser Herz, als er unterwegs mit uns redete, als er uns die Schriften erschloss?" (Lk 24,32)* Der geneigten Leserschaft wird empfohlen, selber nachzulesen, was Lukas vom Geheimnis der Kirche zu sagen weiß. Vielleicht bringt sein ironischer Seitenblick auf einige Deuter des Ostergeschehens uns Schwestern und Brüder zum Schmunzeln, möglicherweise auch über uns selber... In jedem Fall ist allen Leserinnen und Lesern Freude bei der Lektüre dieses Buches zu wünschen.

Reiner Dinger

Verzeichnis der Autoren

Dr. Aku Stephen Antombikums, Wissenschaftlicher Mitarbeiter am Department of Systematic and Historical Theology, Faculty of Theology and Religion, University of Pretoria, antombikums@gmail.com

Morgan D. Bell, Doktorand in Systematischer Theologie an der Toronto School of Theology, University of Toronto, morgan.bell@mail.utoronto.ca

Eckhart Chan, Doktorand an der Oxford University, eckhart.chan@oriel.ox.ac.uk

Dr. Rainer Dinger, Landeskirchenrat i.R., rainerdinger@t-online.de

Dr. Cornelis Christiaan den Hertog, Dozent für öffentliche Theologie (einschl. Ethik) und Systematische Theologie an der Theologischen Universität Apeldoorn, ccdenhertog@tua.nl

Dr. Joe Kauslick, Mitarbeiter an der Boston University School of Theology, jmkaus@bu.edu

Dr. Enoch Kuo, Wiss. Mitarbeiter, Department of Religion, Princeton University, ekuo@princeton.edu

Dr. Cees Jan Smits, Pastor in Papendrecht / Niederlande, ceesjansmits@gmail.com

Jared Stacy, Doktorand in Theologischer Ethik an der University of Aberdeen, j.stacy.20@abdn.ac.uk

Frank Della Torre II, Doktorand in Systematischer Theologie an der Baylor University, St. Waco / Texas, Frank_DellaTorre1@baylor.edu